Left Foreign Policy

Left Foreign Policy

An Organizer's Guide

Matt L. Drabek

Base and Superstructure Press
Iowa City, Iowa

iv

Cover Photo by Bonifacio Pontonio from FreeImages.

ISBN 978-1-7370094-0-5 (paperback)

To everyone attending their first meeting of a leftist group and looking to get involved.

Contents

Introduction

As a college freshman – shortly after September 11, 2001 – I had my first taste of political activism. A motley crew of activists organized a months-long peace camp on the campus of Indiana University in Bloomington, Indiana. As a teenager who grew up in deeply conservative rural Indiana, I had never seen anything like this. The organizers were townies, hipsters, students, anarchists, punks, people experiencing homelessness, and every other group pushed to the margins in my hometown. Conversations were eclectic and engaging, if sometimes frustratingly unfocused. We shared in common the desire to stamp out war and prejudice against our Muslim and Sikh neighbors, uniting around a specific goal: organizing against the War in Afghanistan, which would come to be the longest war in U.S. history. But we also united over concerns closer to home – problems of homelessness, lack of winter shelter, and predatory landlords. We weaved together events happening 7,000 miles from home with those happening 7 blocks from home, showing how the U.S. could put the money it spends conquering the Middle East to better use conquering basic needs in the wealthiest nation on Earth.

These were rich, valuable experiences. The conversations I had and the things I witnessed – including police harassment of the camp and its members – set me on a path to a lifetime of leftist organizing. But the peace camp also provided lessons in the shortcomings of activist movements, particularly anti-war activism. While our conversations were rich and informative, they were also narrow. Many of the people involved in the camp attended *every* demonstration in our Indiana college town. We learned from each other, but we didn't change many minds, win many converts, or have much impact beyond enthusiastic activist circles. The peace camp forged alliances with people experiencing homelessness, but it never built on these gains.

Leftists must learn to take these experiences – these focused, community-building events centered around activist circles – and broaden them to more people and larger communities. How do we use democratic and inclusive principles to expand our circles? How do we do so without getting bogged down in endless deliberation and process? And how does organizing play a role? I refuse to believe the 'usual suspects' in activist circles – the people who attend every demonstration or rally – are so different from the rest of the world that we can't find ways to broaden our efforts. How do we apply lessons from world events and activist actions to build larger, more sustained communities and more effective actions?

Many years later – in late 2019 and early 2020 – I volunteered for the Bernie Sanders presidential campaign. It was an odd move for me, my first presidential campaign as a volunteer. All my previous activist action focused on grassroots, issue-based campaigns and political education. As a Sanders volunteer, I knocked doors in Iowa City, Iowa and had conversations with people in my neighborhood. The campaign volunteer work finished on the night of the Iowa caucuses in February 2020. Iowa caucus-goers jam into a room with their neighbors, spending about two hours in close debate over the best presidential candidate for the Democratic Party. Iowans do it every four years – or *did*, as the case might soon be – taking on an outsized role in U.S. democracy. As a campaign volunteer, I mingled with a nearly 800-strong crowd at the Iowa Memorial Union on the University of Iowa campus, all of them people who lived in a roughly half-mile area on the north side of Iowa City. Joining me were volunteers from nearly a dozen campaigns – from the highly organized and competitive Sanders, Pete Buttigieg, and Elizabeth Warren campaigns to the marginal campaigns of Tulsi Gabbard, Andrew Yang, and – at least at my caucus site – Joe Biden.

A woman a bit older than me asked me a few questions about Bernie's ideas on foreign policy and national security. She was deciding between Sanders and Amy Klobuchar, a rising candidate at the time. Like me, she opposed U.S. military interventionism. She pointed out that Klobuchar –

like Sanders, and in fact like many of the Democratic candidates –
supported cutting the military budget[1]. She saw it as an encouraging sign,
but she also wanted to know what the candidates were doing on issues of
cyber-security. She struggled to differentiate the various candidates from
one another, a challenge many leftists would find surprising. She was a
well-informed voter – perhaps an unusually well-informed one. But
there's nothing unusual about this conversation. Hundreds of thousands
of people share her concerns. Sadly, however, this point would be the *end*
of the conversation for many on the left. Many leftists – even leftists in
activist and organizing circles – wouldn't know how to respond.

That's a problem. Collectively, leftists know they're against wars and
bloated military budgets. And they can connect this opposition to
preventing casualties of war. However, many leftists think of themselves
as *different* from liberals, whether it's merely a matter of degree or one of
kind. The trouble is that this difference is more difficult to pinpoint than
one might imagine. Many liberals – even moderates like Klobuchar –
match leftists in many policy details, or they come close enough to
matching for the casual observer. Leftists therefore don't have steady
means for distinguishing their own foreign policy views from those of
moderate or liberal Democrats. Nor do they have even a broad narrative
of how their anti-war attitudes connect to domestic policy and set their
views apart from fundamentally pro-capital views. Furthermore, though
these conversations are oddly ritualized and stylized, the ones I had with
Iowa caucus-goers aren't much different from the sorts of conversations
people have about politics with family, friends, and neighbors.

Why does this happen? Why can't leftists have good policy
conversations with a wide range of voters? Sometimes I think about the
contrast between these two kinds of conversations: the first with anti-war
comrades and the second with curious and questioning liberals. The
former is important, affirmative, and fulfilling. I feel great about the
conversations and learn from each one. But the latter is probably even *more*

---

[1]   https://www.militarytimes.com/news/pentagon-congress/2019/11/18/military-times-
questionnaire-sen-amy-klobuchar/; https://www.washingtonpost.com/graphics/politics/policy-
2020/foreign-policy/defense-budget/. Last accessed July 27, 2020.

important, and it's downright *necessary* for good organizing, of both the electoral and movement-based types. For leftists, every substantive conversation with a political liberal, political moderate, or politically disaffected worker is a potential breakthrough or a missed opportunity. We can use these conversations to build interest in our organizations and movements.

While conversations with the disaffected are probably the most important, it's worth pausing to consider, in particular, some of the attitudes on the left toward political liberals. Some leftists tend to dismiss these sorts of conversations – conversations like the one I had with an Iowa caucus-goer. People performing leftism on social media, in particular, dismiss these sorts of conversations. Instead, they prefer conversations like the ones at the peace camp – conversations that re-affirm their identities as leftists. As for the woman who put the questions to me, some leftists would call her a 'lib' – even a 'social fascist.' They'd see her as dishonest or outright inauthentic. But it's not true. She wasn't. She wasn't behaving dishonestly, disingenuously, or as anything other than a curious voter. She's a potential part of any broader leftist coalition, and she could become a regular in leftist spaces[2].

Our conversation had a happier ending. We had a good chat about the need for the U.S. to stop blocking a more pluralistic world. We talked about Bernie's positions on issues of war and peace, but, more importantly, we had a conversation between two people about what *we* would like to see. And I think we both gained something from it: I gained a better understanding of the good intentions of many liberals, and she gained a deeper respect for leftists as people who *do* care about the pragmatics of working from where we are now to a better world. It's through these one-on-one conversations that good organizing is done, and

---

[2] In his book *Hegemony How-To*, Jonathan Matthew Smucker addresses these questions head-on. He points out that leftist groups tend to degenerate into insular subcultures. He focuses in particular on case studies around Occupy Wall Street, where leftist subculture often obscured the real advances leftists made toward starting a national conversation around income inequality. See Smucker 2017. Smucker would've had a field day cataloging examples at the February 2020 Iowa caucus, particularly the 'pep rally' environment the Sanders campaign created. This sort of thing excites many Sanders supporters, but it's a big part of why supporters of other candidates had reservations about Sanders.

it's by educating themselves and one another that organizers begin their work. Unfortunately, I didn't see who she ended up supporting in the caucus. Hopefully she ended up on Team Sanders. But even if she didn't, I hope she crosses paths with the left again down the road. Maybe she'll even join a leftist group like the Democratic Socialists of America (DSA). These results build movements.

No Consensus

The left needs better organizing to build larger and more sustained movements. One reason we're unable to do this is that we have no underlying U.S. left consensus on foreign policy, even at a broad level. From progressives to social democrats to anarchists, communists, and socialists, leftists disagree on: when and how to wage war, when and how to support international trade, when and how to intervene in the affairs of other countries, the respective roles of the state and civic organizations, and even the fundamental nature of how the U.S. should relate to the world. My purpose here is to remedy that situation. It's unsustainable, and it blocks the left from making the kinds of gains it's *almost* ready to make.

The lack of left consensus is hardly new[3]. But what gives the left a new sense of urgency – what shakes leftists from their slumber – is the emergence of a striking *domestic* policy consensus. In the wake of the 2008 Global Recession and movements like Black Lives Matter and Occupy Wall Street, the left set aside internal conflict to reach consensus around a policy agenda based on a philosophical commitment to social democracy. The centerpiece is a single-payer health insurance program such as Pramila Jayapal and Bernie Sanders's Medicare for All proposal. For anti-capitalists this is but an initial step toward socialism, while for social democrats it's a completion of the New Deal and Great Society programs

---

[3] In fact, there's something of a cottage industry of mentioning the lack of consensus. It's especially prevalent in left-wing magazine articles and op-eds. See, for example: https://nplusonemag.com/online-only/online-only/the-lefts-missing-foreign-policy; https://newrepublic.com/article/150317/left-wings-foreign-policy; https://www.nytimes.com/2018/09/17/opinion/democratic-party-cortez-foreign-policy.html. All last accessed June 3, 2020.

of the 1930s through 1960s. But for both – and everyone in between – it all begins with social democratic change.

Equally striking, the left hasn't done so around issues of foreign policy. It consistently opposes the most visible and extreme manifestations of U.S. foreign policy, like the 2003 War in Iraq. And some leftist activists criticize aspects of the deeper Washington bipartisan foreign policy consensus. We'll examine this carefully in Chapter 2. But the left's work lacks a unifying vision and philosophical commitment analogous to social democracy in the domestic realm. While the left appeals to something it *calls* 'international solidarity' or 'social change,' it hasn't yet articulated what this looks like in our world and how to apply it to particular cases. By contrast, leftist organizations like the DSA build entire door-to-door campaigns around domestic policies like Medicare for All. They haven't figured out how to transfer these ideas and operations to the foreign policy realm. How about, for example, a nationwide DSA campaign aimed at building solidarity with workers in Latin America? Imagine if we had one.

There's a deep desire for a left foreign policy program, one it can unite with its domestic policy program. It's this desire I seek to encourage and build. The left wants to turn anti-Imperialism and anti-interventionism into international solidarity for peace. It wants to turn domestic social democracy into international solidarity for labor and against capital. To do these things, the left must start from a structural understanding of the U.S.'s relationship with the world. To have the kinds of meaningful conversation that bring in people and start movements, the left needs a baseline of political education for its members. And it needs a core of members who drive action on the topic. The kind of educational program the left needs will proceed against the background of a shared broader foreign policy vision.

My goal here is to help create that grounding for a left foreign policy consensus. I'll develop it through closely examining U.S. relations with seven carefully selected countries in four regions of the world. These cases reveal – and allow us to further develop – a set of basic foreign policy principles. Through these principles, the left can connect the most visible manifestations of U.S. empire and hegemony to the everyday, less visible actions that form the substance of the Washington bipartisan foreign policy consensus. After the left connects these things, it can present a positive alternative of its own.

Beyond Anti-Imperialism

Another result of the lack of organizing is that the left lacks a basic 'mission statement' on foreign policy, and it needs one. The closest it comes is a generic anti-Imperialism that focuses on political and economic domination and references opposition to the building of colonies and domination of territory by the U.S. In practice, leftists apply this through opposition to war[4]. That's not enough. For the left, foreign policy should be about building working-class movements, both domestic and international. It's about coming together with leftists around the globe to fight capital in all its forms: in the boardroom, on the work floor, and in the political arena. Newer leftists – especially young leftists – see international disparities and inequalities in unique ways, particularly given some of newer uses of social media. They gain a window to things veteran leftists rarely – if ever – see. But they lack the theoretical and practical tools – an integrated leftist approach – to put it into action. They can work together with the broader left to create those tools.

In a brief essay in the ABCs of Socialism – an edited volume from Jacobin founder Bhaskar Sunkara and excellent first source for leftists – Jonah Birch introduced issues of war and peace by citing a 1918 anti-World War I speech by Eugene V. Debs. Debs was the consummate early 20th century leftist – the leader of the Socialist Party of America and winner of almost a million votes in the 1912 and 1920 presidential elections. Debs vigorously denounced World War I, and he later ended up in prison because of it. His problem with the war? It was a bloodbath ordered by world leaders for 'conquest and plunder,' as Debs put it[5]. As Birch writes, for Debs the "message to workers was a simple one: their

---

[4] There have been attempts to draw on leftist theorists like V.I. Lenin to expand anti-Imperialism into a full 'mission statement.' See, for example, Awad and bean 2020, particularly pp. 5-6. Awad and bean use 'anti-Imperialism' broadly, which is fine. But for more typical uses of the term, something broader is needed.
[5] https://www.archives.gov/publications/prologue/2017/winter/debs-canton. Last accessed July 27, 2020.

enemy was not...the working-class soldiers they were being shipped off to murder; it was the rulers, on both sides, who ordered the troops into battle. It was the capitalists and their representatives in the American and German governments, whose wealth and power gave them control over the fates of millions[6]."

It was indeed a simple message, and it was a correct one in the case of World War I and many wars of imperial conquest and expansion. These ideas underlie a general leftist approach to foreign policy, and one Birch largely endorsed in his essay. It's an approach on which foreign policy is an expression – an outgrowth – of domestic politics as determined by the need for companies to exploit workers and turn profits. In many cases, this is correct even today. As Birch points out, the U.S. spends hundreds of billions of dollars more on its military than any other nation. It maintains hundreds of military bases overseas[7]. The protection and expansion of American capital plays no small role. The U.S. justifies this approach through appeals to American enthusiasm for democracy, patriotism, and racism[8]. Birch opposes all this. War can only be waged, he concludes, in cases when it's done for the *right reasons*. He gives the example of fighting oppression, citing Abraham Lincoln's opposition to the Mexican-American War of 1848 – a clear case of a war of U.S. aggression – juxtaposed to his fierce prosecution of the Civil War that freed American slaves[9].

While noble and largely correct, none of this – and very little popular left thought – moves beyond the initial anti-Imperialism. It focuses almost entirely on wars of aggression. But here's one simple – and important – way we might move beyond it. Consider again why the U.S. has so many military bases. Yes, it maintains hundreds of overseas bases to fight wars. It also has hundreds of domestic military bases. Do these bases mainly serve as places to train soldiers to fight wars? They certainly perform this function, but it might not be its main function. Towns fight for military bases, and they fight to keep them. Bases bring thousands of jobs and

---

[6] Jonah Birch in Sunkara 2016, p. 106.
[7] Birch in Sunkara 2016, p. 107. See also Vine 2020.
[8] Birch in Sunkara 2016, pp. 107-109.
[9] Birch in Sunkara 2016, pp. 112-113.

improve the overall economy of the towns where they're located. In fact, U.S. military bases are one of the last remaining federal jobs programs in the country. They're one of the last remaining such programs not roundly criticized by the U.S. right-wing and – increasingly – even moderate and liberal Americans.

To build a consensus – one that includes new leftist activists and reaches even more people – we must move beyond basic anti-Imperialism. Not because it's wrong. It isn't. But anti-Imperialism doesn't help us build a positive program. It doesn't get us past introductory meetings, reactions against immediate crises and wars, and a wide variety of demonstrations and pickets that – while useful for building enthusiasm and participation – rarely accomplish much unless they're a part of a much broader program of theory and action. In some cases, like the conversation I had at the Iowa caucus, it doesn't even get us through first meetings. To build something more sustained and useful, we must show how U.S. action abroad connects to our world at home and how we can build ties with working-class people around the globe.

The Limits and Potential of Consensus

There will always be disagreement on the left. Disagreement can be healthy and productive, and it's an expected and welcome consequence of the left's commitment to democratic deliberation and inclusion. As with the leftist domestic policy consensus around the short-term pursuit of social democracy, a leftist foreign policy consensus will likely be a soft one. What I'll do is lay out enough of a program and enough criteria for guiding movements, having one-on-one and group conversations with new and potential leftists, and judging electoral candidates. Each reader should come away able to do these things. As for the deep questions of socialist theory and practice – whether and how to transition from international social democracy to full socialism? That'll mostly remain in the air and – hopefully – on the table.

What I seek here is neither utopia nor an end point. Rather, it's a starting point. It's a baseline understanding of how the U.S. relates to the world, the U.S.'s drives and motivations in those relations, and a deeper criticism of U.S. foreign policy. From such a starting point, even the novice leftist should be ready to discuss and develop a leftist foreign policy to stand alongside the left's social democratic domestic policy. The reader, too, can have a discussion with anyone attending a political meeting or caucus. While it sounds simple and basic, it's much more difficult than it seems. But it's also incredibly useful.

This means that while the project is limited in various ways, it's also full of potential and, ultimately, it's a generative engine for building movements and achieving change. Many long-time organizers – myself certainly included – recognize the revolving door of people who attend one or two meetings and then disappear. Lots of people – especially young people – are looking for a narrative and for ways to get involved. Foreign policy is a crucial aspect of this, particularly in times of war but even during times of (relative) peace. War always lurks just beneath the surface. Beyond that, the kinds of things the left does to build a coherent foreign policy will critically assist even with domestic policy goals. Mass member-based groups working for single-payer health insurance have a lot to learn from how other nations implemented nationalized health care or universal health insurance. Groups working to organize tenants or workers in the U.S. can learn how organizations elsewhere build and maintain themselves. And they can build connections and bonds of solidarity with the workers in other countries connected to the same company in our system of globalized and financialized capitalism.

These links are a gold mine for movement building both internationally and domestically. And they're waiting for nothing more than cultivation and organization. Thus, working on foreign policy serves multiple purposes for the left, purposes both substantive and practical. Foreign policy should not – *cannot* – be the narrow realm of experts, though experts are important. It must be a core part of a leftist program, helping the left draw in and retain new members while also building links required for an international coalition of workers and other marginalized groups. The left can learn from – and grow with – grassroots workers' movements throughout the world.

Building a Narrative

In Redemption – an episode of *Star Trek: The Next Generation* – Captain Jean-Luc Picard of the United Federation of Planets had an opportunity to intervene in a civil war among the alien Klingon Empire. While all civil wars are messy and complicated, this one seemed relatively clear. One side of the civil war was clearly correct according to Klingon law, and its victory presented the best chance for the greater good. The other side – the one in the wrong, legally – was supported and supplied by the Romulan Star Empire, an enemy of the Federation. The situation presents us with close to a 'best case' for foreign intervention: an alignment of the law with the greater good and the apparent best interest of the intervening force.

And yet Picard refused to intervene. He refused on the principled grounds that interference is illegitimate and can lead to unintended consequences. It can do so even when a benevolent force like the Federation is doing the intervening. However, Picard stood on principle and law alone. He lacked deeper reasons for his refusal, deeper justifications or movements. Picard operated in the world of military diplomacy, which relies on formal hierarchies rather than popular movements. Ultimately, his principles failed due to this lack of deeper support or movements. By the end of the episode, Picard inserted himself as the strategic director of an entire side of a civil war.

In the end, all worked out for the best. But the show's writers used farcical means to get there, writing a classic *deux ex machina* plot resolution. In the episode, an Android named Data saved the day due to his superhuman abilities, teaching viewers a lesson against discrimination to boot. All ended well, and the crew of the *Enterprise* lived on for another episode. Of course, this kind of thing only works in fiction. In the real world, we don't have Androids or anyone else with supernatural abilities. We know our abilities are all too human, even when our intentions are good.

The U.S. political establishment excels at creating these kinds of fictional narratives even in the real world. It does so even though even many of the favorable conditions available in the world of *Star Trek* are absent from the world of U.S. intervention. U.S. politics builds narratives of its own where the left's foreign policy views aren't able to win or be successful. One important task of this book will be to shed light on this phenomenon and build our collective ability to work through these false narratives and create alternative narratives. In the real world, violating non-interventionist principles fails, and while Picard is a great captain – and important teacher – for much of the show, he certainly wasn't in this particular episode. This book will – among other things – provide readers with a stronger and more coherent anti-interventionist narrative with positive alternatives to intervention.

Picard's failure reveals an overall approach to foreign policy issues on the left. Regardless of the intentions of particular actors on the policy stage – politicians, experts, et al. – foreign relations have an underlying structure. And it's difficult to break out of this structure. The U.S. left recognized this long ago, and the knowledge is tacit even with novice leftists. As the magazine Jacobin put it in the title of a special issue: War is a racket[10]. The specific point, of course, is that war often earns profits for certain groups of capitalists. But more broadly, it means that there are underlying interests involved in foreign relations just as there are in domestic relations. To the U.S. leftist familiar with how profits hold us back from achieving single-payer health insurance, the point will sound familiar. Part of the left's task on foreign policy is to unearth underlying narrow interests and shift focus to our broad, collective interests.

A real-world Picard would have failed in part because a single heroic individual – no matter how well-placed or brave – can't override these interests on their own. Much like the domestic politics of health care or minimum wages, foreign policy has to be a collective, democratic process. We're in it together. There's a common misconception that foreign policy is special, unique – that it's the realm of the expert, even if domestic politics are a collective project. It's an important goal of this book to defeat that misconception. Foreign policy *also* requires careful deliberation around collective interests. It requires a framework of international social democracy to meet the left's conception of domestic social democracy.

---

[10] https://jacobinmag.com/issue/war-is-a-racket. Last accessed July 27, 2020.

The Book's Argument and Chapters

The book is divided into two parts. Part I provides the reader with a basic orientation. It helps move the reader from where they are – the left's currently incomplete foreign policy – to where they need to be – ready to build an integrated left foreign policy vision. We'll start in Chapter 1 with an overview of left-wing and foreign policy terminology. Many readers enter these debates bewildered, assured that something is wrong with the world but unfamiliar with the paths already blazed by the left. The chapter defines 'left' in terms of anti-capitalism, using the left's orientation against capitalism and in favor of a socialist alternative to distinguish it from liberal and progressive viewpoints. The chapter also provides an overview of the two most common viewpoints about foreign policy – realism and liberal internationalism – and situates a left foreign policy as an approach distinct from both of these viewpoints.

Chapter 2 lays out the four basic principles of a left foreign policy: international solidarity, anti-interventionism, pluralism, and fighting global capital. It defends these four principles as the interconnected tools needed to build better left movements. These principles form much of the handbook for left foreign policy organizing. The chapter explains each principle in the context of examples of U.S. foreign policy actions. And it shows why the principles will help us clarify a left foreign policy. It provides a blueprint and roadmap for close analysis of future issues and cases. The chapter emphasizes how the four principles work together: international solidarity allows leftists to build bridges between different left groups, anti-interventionism provides space for leftists in other countries to build their own movements, pluralism gives leftists throughout the world a chance to succeed, and fighting global capital brings us together for a shared leftist battle.

Chapter 3 closely examines the debate over open borders with respect to immigration. It argues for open borders as an important goal of the U.S. left in line with the four basic principles. The chapter makes the case that it's critical for the U.S. left to build relationships with immigrant workers, and an open borders policy is the best way to make it safe for immigrant workers to join labor unions and leftist movements. U.S. immigrants already have organic bonds with working-class people in other countries.

By nurturing and tapping into these bonds, the U.S. left can build the new relationships needed to fight global capital at all points in the global supply chain. Open borders are the best path to building these relationships because only through free movement in and out of the country will immigrant workers feel fully empowered to join labor unions and broader movements.

Part II moves on to consider case studies of U.S. relations with nations in four regions of the world. Chapter 4 examines U.S. relations with the Latin American nations of Venezuela and Bolivia, focusing on international solidarity and anti-interventionism. It lays out what the U.S. left can learn from experimentation in popular democracy, and it carefully documents the explicit and implicit ways the U.S. blocks positive developments. The chapter lays out what the U.S. left can learn from building organic links with popular groups in Venezuela and Bolivia. It argues that the best way to encourage democratic movements in the region is to resist U.S. intervention. The primary lessons come from Venezuela's communal council system and Bolivia's grassroots, Indigenous movements. The chapter carefully documents both the explicit and implicit ways the U.S. blocks positive developments.

Chapter 5 examines the special challenges of the Middle East region through U.S. support for war in Syria and colonialism in Israel/Palestine. It argues that an effective anti-interventionist stance is key to reducing the harm done by the U.S. and that a more pluralistic world is one that would benefit both the region and the U.S. left. Israel – the regional hegemonic power and a key U.S. ally – currently dominates the region. The chapter uses the region as a case study in anti-interventionism and pluralism, in particular. It carefully documents U.S. funding for war in Syria and colonialism in Israel/Palestine, arguing that an effective anti-interventionist stance is key to reducing the harm done by the U.S. and freeing up space for a wider range of powers in the region. A more pluralistic world where power moves beyond the U.S. and its allies would benefit the Middle East region and the U.S. left. And the U.S. left itself has much to learn from pan-Arab resistance movements.

Chapter 6 examines contemporary issues in East Asia, using a fading North Korea and a surging China as contrast cases. These contrast cases highlight, in particular, the basic principles of pluralism and fighting global capital. While the chapter argues that the North Korean state has few merits, it shows that a more pluralistic world would better allow North Koreans to work through their current struggles and achieve a more democratic society. It carefully documents how U.S. pressure encourages, rather than discourages, problems. It argues that organic bonds with workers are particularly important in China, which is key to the global supply chain. Alliances between U.S. and Chinese workers can be extremely effective in fighting global capital.

Chapter 7 examines U.S. relations with sub-Saharan Africa, focusing on U.S. relations with Nigeria as a representative case of how the U.S. facilitates the extraction of land, labor, and natural resources in countries at a different stage of development. The chapter draws an analogy to a different kind of resource extraction happening in the U.S., a comparison that will allow readers to see the link between the extraction of resources abroad and at home. By using only a single example, the chapter has space to go into greater depth on these issues. It introduces the key terms of 'primitive accumulation' and 'accumulation by dispossession' to explain U.S. policy in the region. And it connects these forces to analogous forces in domestic U.S. politics, like rent and contract labor.

Finally, the book concludes with attention to how U.S. leftists – especially new and enthusiastic young leftists – can put these principles into practice through their own discussions. The conclusion focuses on key U.S. interventions in Serbia and Afghanistan as cases. Together, this work provides a map for future consolidation and development of a left domestic and foreign policy agenda. The conclusion provides additional ways to build international solidarity movements and highlights stories from my own background in leftist organizing, using the stories as a way to encourage readers in their conversations with other activists. We'll also look at practical ways to connect and expand on this work.

About and By the Left

I switch rather freely in this book between the third person ('the left' or 'the U.S. left') and the first-person plural ('us' or 'we'), using one or the other where it seems most appropriate. Readers may have already noticed this. The reality of the situation is that there are many lefts in the U.S., and many people in the U.S. with partial or total attachment to the term 'left.' This situation will be a key focus in the first chapter. And so, the unitary phrasing will remain a constant issue. One challenge of writing this book is that it's about the left, and I myself am a member of the left with a particular political background and political aims. And while I will advocate for my own particular views where appropriate, I'm also writing in an ecumenical way that encourages internal discussion, debate, and, at times, *dissent*. I've long been a part of the most heated internal left debates over the wisdom of particular foreign policy approaches and interventions, with intervention in places like Serbia and Afghanistan perhaps the most heated. I'll argue later that those interventions were misguided, and I'll do so using the principles contained in this book. But even readers who disagree with me on particular applications of the principles should find the principles themselves both correct and helpful.

In addition to our plurality of left movements, we have a plurality of goals. One key goal of this book is to explore a certain problem on the left: the lack of a coherent foreign policy orientation and program. But a second key goal – perhaps even a more important goal – is to provide the reader with a helpful orientation toward having the kinds of discussions I had at the Iowa caucuses and many of us have at political meetings, especially the meetings of new political groups. I hope this book proves helpful to the reader in clarifying their own thoughts, and I hope it provides a starting point for forming their own reading and study groups. This goal places the book in something of the tradition of, say, Labor Notes's *Secrets of a Successful Organizer*[11] or Jane McAlevey's *No Shortcuts*[12]. Both of those books serve as manuals for organizers focused on one-on-one conversations with people new to popular movements. I hope this book can – to some extent – serve the same purpose for the reader.

For my part, I've evolved in many ways in my foreign policy thinking over the years. While I was an opponent of war very early in life – radicalized, one might say, by the War in Afghanistan – my early

---

[11] Bradbury, et al. 2016.
[12] McAlevey 2018.

opposition to war wasn't especially reflective. In seeing conflicts in the years since 2001 – both newer conflicts like the 2003 War in Iraq and reading in more detail about earlier conflicts like the War in Vietnam – I've come to confirm more deeply in my thinking the sheer folly of U.S. interventionism in almost all its forms. Near the beginning of this evolutionary process, it's incredibly unlikely I'd have been able to carry on a conversation about foreign policy beyond a knee-jerk reaction against the use of U.S. military might against less powerful opponents. I hope now to be able to tell a much richer story about how the left can oppose current U.S. intervention while developing the structures and threads of an alternative within the spaces of our current world.

Finally, my methods in writing this book differ in certain respects from the final product itself. I began more from the case studies in Part II than from the principles of Part I. That's to say I started with examples and only later drew out broad themes and lessons. But in writing this book, I start with the lessons. I'd encourage readers to bridge that gap by doing a bit of both. Readers may find it best to start by skimming the basic principles in Part I, carefully reading through the case studies in Part II, and then arriving afresh at the principles in Part I, connecting them with more concreteness to the case studies. This is, I think, the best way to arrive at the right method and get the most out of the book. From there, organizers can begin building the movements they need to create international social democracy.

Part I

Finding Our Way

Is a photograph that is not sharp a picture of a person at all? Is it
even always an advantage to replace a picture that is not
sharp by one that is? Isn't one that isn't sharp
often just what we need?

Ludwig Wittgenstein, *Philosophical Investigations*

Chapter 1

"What is the Left?" and "What is Foreign Policy?"

The last thing the left needs is another debate over who counts as a leftist. Instead, we need to swear off boundary policing to improve our spaces, especially our online spaces. Boundary policing turns people off, people like the potential leftist I spoke with at the Iowa caucus. Few people are interested in joining a pissing contest, and we shouldn't be interested in holding one. These contests are a major reason why we have – at least on paper – more than two dozen socialist parties in the U.S. We can't get together to discuss a common vision until we let people enter our spaces, learn, make mistakes, and then improve. Failing to create these inclusive spaces for development and growth leads to these dozens of splinter groups.

Many readers moved to the left in the time since 2016. People in this camp are dissatisfied with our current world and want to make it better. Online quizzes that tell you whether you're an anarchist, anarcho-communist, anarcho-syndicalist, Marxist, Leninist, Marxist-Leninist, Maoist, Marxist-Leninist-Maoist, Trotskyist, democratic socialist, or just regular old socialist do interest some people. I like these quizzes, too! Sometimes they even help us explore subtle differences in leftist theory in fun and informative ways. But they're mostly good for passing the time. They're entertainment. We have more important things to do, and new leftists want to move beyond historical minutiae.

And yet we need a coherent, united leftist program. We need to reach decisions, build a platform, and proudly defend that platform. When we begin from a stance of open-mindedness to new members and new ideas, we do so with the understanding that this method achieves *results*. We can come together and lay out together what a leftist program looks like. We can build consensus around which foreign policy views are acceptable and which aren't. But to get there, we need an initial understanding of what counts as 'leftist,' and then we need to help people reach it. Leftism can't amount to simply *anything* to the left of the Republican Party. Nor can it simply count as anything to the left of some generic, vague 'moderate Democrat' – perhaps Joe Manchin, a Democratic Senator from West Virginia. That's *far* too loose, and it leaves open too many issues leftists settled long ago. There's less political distance between a moderate Democrat and Donald Trump than there is between the same moderate Democrat and a socialist.

Our key problem at the outset is that we're not yet creating an open space for discussion, and we don't have a good, shared leftist background from which to begin. Our terms are fuzzy and squishy. We use them without confidence. Or, even worse, we use them with confidence but *wrongly*. They don't tell us – and new leftists – much about the left and its aims. We know the left includes communists, socialists, and anarchists. But does it include social democrats, progressives, liberals, and others? To find their way about, readers – particularly new leftists – need clear distinctions, distinctions that clear up the muddied waters. In this chapter, we'll work through basic leftist ideas in sufficient depth to give us a starting point. From there, readers will be prepared to talk with potential leftists and work toward building a left foreign policy.

The Left

For the last couple of years, I've been involved with the Iowa City Tenants Union. We hold monthly meetings and canvass local tenants to build members, fight landlords, and create better housing policy. We talk with tenants one-on-one and in small groups to discuss their housing problems and the ways we can build power together. Tenants know from experience that landlords get paid for owning things rather than working.

Many hold basic leftist intuitions and sentiments based on these experiences – whether they explicitly name those intuitions or not – but they haven't developed them. Would we restrict meetings to people who endorse a leftist political program? Would we *require* each new person to endorse a public, democratically managed housing system designed to squeeze the landlord class? Of course not. We want people to get there, but we have to *help* them get there. We can't demand they already be there when we find them. Good organizing involves meeting people where they are and working with them at each step. Most tenants begin this work unfamiliar with housing jargon and with how we can use public housing as a tool for class conflict and victory over landlords. The same is true of direct action campaigns, usually built around applying pressure to landlords to, e.g., return security deposits. Many tenants begin with the notion that the law is there to protect their interests. They've got a lot to learn. Only through shared struggle do they learn tenants can only win by working together democratically as a group rather than relying on the law or the political system.

There's a balancing act at work here. The U.S. left needs to remain open to new members. This requires open-endedness and flexibility. But it must distinguish itself from other ideas and forces, particularly the Democratic Party and the capitalist interests it serves, from military contractors to landlords. This requires analytical clarity and rigor. What holds for organizing tenants also holds for organizing workers and organizing people around foreign policy and solidarity. People join unions and participate in workplace actions when they're comfortable and feel welcome. They need to see the link between their experience and the work. Good organizers start with workers and tenants sympathetic to leftist ideas. But they work with them from the beginning, making sure they learn what they need to learn and pick up the ability to work through leftist ideas confidently. Everyone attending a meeting should feel comfortable, and everyone should move closer to leftist ideology. This requires both a clear program and openness to well-meaning liberals, progressives, or people without a fixed identification.

So, let's try our best to define the left, keeping these things in mind:

Leftists stand against capitalism and want to replace it with democratic ownership and control of the world's economic system. The left favors economic democracy as a replacement for the system of economic authoritarianism and oligarchy we call 'capitalism.'

I think this is by far the best quick summary of what unites the left. At its core, the left believes ordinary people can and should run their own lives – particularly their economic lives – because all these areas – particularly the economy – deeply influence all areas of culture and politics. And it's the concept of 'left' I'll work with in this book – the line dividing leftist views from non-leftist ones. As we work through similar and/or competing terms – progressive, social democrat, et al. – we'll judge these terms against the standard in the paragraph above. Most leftists refer to economic democracy as 'socialism,' or perhaps 'democratic socialism.' But even that's something we shouldn't police too closely at the outset. Marxist sociologist Erik Olin Wright helpfully points out in the preface to his book *Envisioning Real Utopias*[13] that the term 'socialism' alienates some people. Others find it muddled or confusing. If so, that's fair. I hope each leftist comes to embrace the term, but we need not start with it. What we need is the underlying idea that people should control their work. From there, we can establish socialism as much through action as through definition.

This all makes for a great starting point. But a definition and its application are separate issues. Even a well-formed definition leaves open many questions of application. For one, leftists differ on issues of how to enact short-term change. We differ, that is to say, in terms of the methods we use. Some want to work on electoral paths to power. For some leftists, this means working within the Democratic Party to push it to the left. For others, it means forming – yet another! – third party. And for still others, it means adopting a hybrid route. One recently trending idea is to form a 'party surrogate' that would work both within and outside of the Democratic Party. And then, some leftists avoid the electoral route completely. They want to focus on organizing tenants, workers, and others

---

[13] Olin Wright 2019.

dispossessed and/or marginalized by capitalism. They want to build movements first, and then worry about elections later (or not at all!).

I'll remain mostly agnostic on those questions, at least for now. We all have thoughts about them. For present purposes, I'll set those aside. In their book *Poor People's Movements*[14], Frances Fox Piven and Richard Cloward helpfully point out – and defend through careful argumentation – the thesis that partisan electoral politics typically come at the *end* of movements rather than at the *beginning*. Change rarely begins with a political party or an electoral campaign, and people rarely begin from that point, either. At least not most successful activists. Rather, they start by taking action – by rallying around some cause important to them. Formalizing this action through political participation requires careful deliberation with a group of people one trusts. Had there been a strong prior social democratic and socialist movement, for example, I suspect the Bernie Sanders campaign would have been more successful[15]. At the very least, I think it would have been more resistant to the kind of electoral maneuvering the more moderate Democratic candidates pushed through when they collectively dropped out after the South Carolina primary and endorsed the successful campaign of Joe Biden. And so, I'm very sympathetic to Piven and Cloward.

Back to the Dreaded Question: Who Counts as a Leftist?

We know that even with solid definitions, we still have work to do. But solid definitions help us clarify many issues. Let's return to the issue of 'the left.' We know the 'radical left' counts as a part of the U.S. left. This includes anarchists, communists, and socialists. But we need to consider other views in more detail. What about progressives? Liberals? Social

---

[14] Piven and Cloward 1979 [1977].

[15] This issue has gotten significant attention from Bernie Sanders supporters since he lost the nomination to Joe Biden in 2020. See, in particular, Day and Uetricht 2020. Day and Uetricht argue in favor of a more electoralist approach, but they do so on pragmatic grounds. They find the Bernie movement wildly successful at building members. I think their argument is much worth consideration. I've addressed it elsewhere: https://baseandsuperstructure.com/bigger-than-bernie-us-left-after-sanders.

democrats? Are they part of the U.S. left? Do they support economic democracy and/or oppose capitalism?

Let's start our discussion of this set of thorny issues with a deeper discussion of progressives and social democrats. 'Progressive' is, in fact, an older term that has roared back in popularity in recent years. For more than a century – from the early 20th century to today – progressive movements stood against capitalist excesses: corruption, monopolies, lack of transparency. Theodore Roosevelt's fight against monopolies and trusts exemplified the progressive movement in U.S. domestic policy in the early 20th century. He started dozens of antitrust suits, using regulation as a sharp tool against capitalist excess. But he did so not to *oppose* capitalism, but rather to *save* capitalism from itself. It's far less clear how progressives handle foreign policy. Insofar as they did hold a coherent foreign policy, historians know Woodrow Wilson as their best case. Wilson's Fourteen Points speech at the end of World War I stands out as a highlight of the policy. In that speech, he advocated for the breakup of European empires and called for local control of territory. On the surface, then, progressives stood against empire and in favor of local autonomy, though even this stance leaves us with some doubts as to how forcefully progressives really opposed empire. We'll revisit these issues in Chapter 2.

The term 'progressive' never completely went out of style. Then it became more popular during the Obama years, especially as a way for Democrats further to the left to distinguish their views from those of moderate Democrats like Bill Clinton. And I think its current use lines up well with its historical one. Today's progressives use the term in various ways – both as a way to distinguish themselves from liberals and as a way to unite themselves with liberals under a big tent organization. By either usage, they end up advocating policies strikingly similar to those of early 20th century progressives. We might consider the case of Elizabeth Warren, likely the best example of a political progressive in the current sense. Her 2020 presidential campaign directly hit all the notes from progressive history. She based her campaign on capitalism's rigged rules and discriminatory policy, opposing these things largely on the grounds that they block the flow of capital through the economy. In response, Warren put together a progressive program for the early 21st century:

breakup the tech monopolies, end corruption and the revolving door between government and industry, open the economy to people of color, trans people, women, and intersections among these groups. All this amounts to textbook progressivism. It's not anti-capitalist, but it advocates for a more humane, sustainable capitalism.

Is progressivism a part of the U.S. left, and is Warren a leftist? Given what we've seen, it's important for leftists to think hard about whether they want to continue organizing under the 'progressive' label. And from our starting point above, we'll probably want to answer those questions 'no' and 'no.' Warren told us she's a "capitalist to my bones[16]," and she's quite right. She *is* a capitalist to her bones. She fights against the abuses and excesses of the capitalist system, not against the capitalist system itself. Warren wants to make capitalism *better*. And she holds this in common with the entire progressive movement. Insofar as progressives accept capitalism in some form, they're not leftists as we laid out the term 'leftist' above. Leftists may want to unclog capitalism's arteries as do progressives, but leftists eventually want to replace it with something better. The left wants to democratize the economy, to restructure ownership and control. But while some of the people who identify as 'progressive' might want this, too, it's inconsistent with how progressivism has played out throughout its history.

I'm afraid the term 'social democrat' has an even more complicated history. At certain places and times – notably Germany's Social Democratic Party in the early 20th century and the UK's Labour Party in the mid-20th century – social democrats were just socialists who embraced a gradual, democratic route to socialism. They built large political parties based around union members in the industrial economy. They wanted to build socialism by winning ever-larger amounts of electoral power, while simultaneously using that electoral power to push the priorities of their union members. Eventually, they wanted to use this power to take over businesses in the name of their workers. And so, in those times and places

---

[16] See, for example, the interview with Warren in The Atlantic for an overview of her vision of capitalism: https://www.theatlantic.com/politics/archive/2018/08/elizabeth-warrens-theory-of-capitalism/568573/. See also Drabek 2021. Last accessed June 25, 2020.

there simply wasn't any hard distinction between social democrats and socialists. Socialists perhaps wanted to eliminate capitalism more quickly, but both wanted it gone. Social democrats *were* socialists in those days.

On this model, social democracy is a transitional stage. It's a stage where we strengthen the standard of living through universal social programs before the deeper socialist transformation. One might think of it through Maslow's hierarchy of needs: first workers organize for social democratic programs meeting everyone's basic needs, and then workers use their political power to push for ownership and control of the very businesses generating products and wealth. The earlier stages of the transition build up the capacity and confidence of workers' movements. Once they see what they can accomplish with things like education and health care, they're ready to take on larger projects.

The trouble is that we have a newer term now for a gradual, democratic route to socialism. That term is 'democratic socialism.' In the U.S., the Democratic Socialists of America (DSA) is probably the best-known group using the term this way. For the DSA, 'democratic socialism' refers to this very system of using worker-based movements to start with social democratic change and follow it through to socialist transformation. Much of the U.S. left media also uses 'democratic socialism' in this way. Readers of *Current Affairs* and *Jacobin* – and their editors Nathan J. Robinson and Bhaskar Sunkara, respectively – find this terrain familiar. Both Robinson and Sunkara wrote recent books on socialism, and they defend precisely this usage. They ground 'democratic socialism' in gradual, democratic change led by workers, and they associate it with the 2020 Bernie Sanders campaign[17].

---

[17] Sunkara 2019, p. 201. Despite repeatedly employing a methodological definition of 'democratic socialism' in his book, even Sunkara occasionally slips and recognizes a more substantive difference between social democracy as a system and democratic socialism as a system. In his recommendations at the end of the book, for example, he follows Erik Olin Wright's definitions when advocating for a transition from 'social democracy' to 'democratic socialism' (pp. 221-223). There's also the much thornier issue of where the actual Bernie Sanders campaign lands on these issues. I don't want to take up too much time and space rehashing Sanders and Sandersism, and so I'll just lay out my own interpretation: Sanders uses 'democratic socialism' to mean something much more like what I mean by 'social democracy' in this book.

Most functioning social democracies in the world today – as well as the political parties operating under that name – focus solely on the public standard of living. They stopped at things like the state ownership of human essentials or – in some cases – key industries[18]. That was enough for them. They long ago dropped any ambition to transition to full socialism. Instead they pivoted away from radical language to pragmatic language, and they shifted their base from the industrial working class to the middle and professional classes. Nations like Finland or Sweden – the cases Bernie Sanders himself cites as potential models for the U.S. – built social democracy on the basis of working-class struggle. But the system itself – the social democracy that resulted – was a class compromise. It addressed the needs and concerns both of workers and of capitalists. For workers, the system provided a high standard of living and access to necessities. For capitalists, it provided a stable system where they maintained ownership and control of the economy and could accumulate capital in peace. A few leftists, in fact, *advocate* for this approach in the short-term. Erik Olin Wright, for example, thinks socialism would run into so many difficulties that it's not a worthwhile short- or medium-term goal[19]. Rather, he leans toward class compromise as the goal while socialists work on changing the underlying legal structure of society.

I'm going to define 'social democracy' in the way people use it to describe nations like Finland or Sweden. In a social democracy, the state provides everyone with basic necessities. This includes things like education, health care, and housing. And the state provides these things through a combination of taxation, regulation, and outright public ownership. The social democratic state provides these things as an *end*

---

[18] A few socialists, e.g., deBoer 2020, go one step further and define 'socialism' specifically as the destruction of markets. Others believe 'market socialism' is possible. I remain neutral in that debate.

[19] In Olin Wright 2019, pp. 44-46, Olin Wright uses the term 'social democrat' in an even softer way than how I'm using it here. Olin Wright thinks of a social democrat in roughly the way I think of a 'progressive' – someone who wants better programs for poorer people and regulation of capitalism thorough enough to give it clean rules and promote the good flow of capital. Part of his motivation here appears to be what he describes as the structural difficulties of transitioning from social democracy to socialism. He thinks the capitalist system sets up legal and structural barriers making such a transition nearly impossible in the current environment.

point rather than as the early stage of a transition to socialism. Indeed, the social democratic class compromise itself is about *ending* class conflict, not expanding it by building socialism. The core areas of the economy – where workers generate value appropriated by capitalists, such as the manufacturing or service sectors – remains largely under private ownership and control. Distinguishing between social democracy and socialism in this way provides us with a great deal of analytical clarity. It also gives us a tool for analyzing nations as they transition – or *don't* transition – from the former to the latter.

Countries don't always fit cleanly into one box or the other. And so, there are exceptions to how social democracies behave. Leftist theorists *love* discussing these exceptions. For example, they spill gallons of ink discussing the Swedish Meidner Plan as an anti-capitalist blueprint within a social democracy[20]. The Swedes wanted to pass a law requiring companies of a certain size and type to pay a special tax into a fund controlled by workers. Workers would operate it via their unions. And – over time – the fund would build, eventually hitting an amount large enough for the union to *buy* the company from its private owners. In theory, this establishes socialism purely via market transactions. It's a good case for discussion. However, one reason everyone talks about it is that it's one of the *only* examples. Using social democracy to get to actual socialism is, in fact, quite *rare*. In typical cases, social democracy offers a much more tepid anti-capitalism, if it offers an anti-capitalism at all. Far more common is the 'social democratic' party that works with capitalists to roll back social democratic programs! This is exactly where the German Social Democratic and UK Labour Parties ended up by the 1990s.

The Less Well-Defined

It's important for the U.S. left to come to grips with these labels. But we must remember that many people don't start from a set ideology – many don't know precisely what they mean by the labels, and some don't

---

[20] One might cite dozens – perhaps hundreds – of examples here. Jacobin's coverage from 2017 is fairly representative: https://www.jacobinmag.com/2017/08/sweden-social-democracy-meidner-plan-capital. Last accessed June 25, 2020.

use the labels at all. Some approach politics from specific concerns, often grounded in their experiences as workers and tenants. The U.S. left wants to reach people grappling with serious social problems, including things like: racism, lack of health insurance, unemployment, et al. While each of these issues relates to capitalism in deep, systemic ways, people don't start by considering those relations. They start by reflecting on how they've been harmed. And they likely have a general feeling that the current system isn't working for them and their family. When a new person walks in to a political meeting – or a leftist invites them to one – it's critical to have a story about how those personal experiences relate to social forces. And while labels can be helpful, labels don't substitute for the hard work of connecting these things together. The 2020 racial justice protests across the U.S. serve as a key example of all of this. The protests grew out of many things, including general anger, fear, mass unemployment, and the increasing realization that the system is stacked against young black Americans. Building a narrative about the larger social forces at play – and connecting that narrative to daily life – was key to the success (or failure) of the protests.

Young Americans increasingly identify as socialists[21]. But they do so whether or not they have strong views about the *term* 'socialism.' Many readers of this book might be young people without settled views on the term 'socialism.' They know the system has failed them, and they know they need something better. 'Socialism' stands – if nothing else – as a powerful marker for 'something better.' It's easy to dismiss all this as dilettantism, as young people playing with labels and identities. More skeptical readers might think young people will grow out of it and focusing on them wastes organizers' time. However, this attitude misses what young people are doing and the issues they're struggling with. It misses a series of great organizing opportunities, and it ignores the many things young people bring to the table. I think young people are lashing out against capitalism. And I think they have at least some notion of what the world *should* look like, even if it needs a lot of development. Further

---

[21] See, for example, Gallup's work: https://news.gallup.com/poll/268766/socialism-popular-capitalism-among-young-adults.aspx. Last accessed June 27, 2020.

survey research, for example, shows young people moving noticeably to the left on a wide range of issues, such as Medicare for All and free college[22].

They're reaching toward leftism, and they need good organizers to help them along. Many – including some readers of this book! – will also become organizers themselves. The U.S. left can – should, *must* – encourage and support this development. They'll work through fits and starts and stumbles along the way. And organizers have to be there to support them. Their leftism emerges in odd ways, sometimes in concerning ways. Electorally, newer leftists took a wide range of stances in 2020. Most who voted chose Bernie Sanders in the 2020 primaries. That's hardly a surprise. A few voted for Elizabeth Warren, though support for Warren was more concentrated among people with graduate degrees and higher incomes. A few more alienated and disaffected young leftists chose candidates like Tulsi Gabbard or Andrew Yang. Of course, quite a few didn't vote at all, particularly those with lower incomes and/or working-class backgrounds.

Some are rough around the edges, sometimes in concerning ways. They do things on social media many people find off-putting. And sometimes people find those things off-putting for good reasons. Posting 'snake emojis' directed at Elizabeth Warren stands out as something of a low point[23]. Organizers shouldn't encourage this kind of thing, but they should understand where it's coming from. There's anger out there, and it's justified anger. Good political education and development can redirect justified anger toward better outlets. Some young people identify with terms like 'liberal' or 'progressive,' terms that don't necessarily align well to their actual experience and outlook. Organizers must remain open to this and avoid dismissing them as 'libs' or in some other derisive way. With education and shared struggle they can match their labels to their

---

[22] See this Harris Poll research and Axios visualization: https://www.axios.com/exclusive-poll-young-americans-embracing-socialism-b051907a-87a8-4f61-9e6e-0db75f7edc4a.html.   Last accessed June 27, 2020.

[23] See Vox's coverage: https://www.vox.com/culture/2020/1/15/21067331/warren-is-a-snake-hashtag-explained. See also Drabek 2021. Last accessed June 27, 2020.

anti-capitalist sentiments. For organizers, openness and understanding are key.

And so, I think we have a good starting point. The U.S. left contains a small pool of explicit anti-capitalists. This includes people who identify somewhere in the anarchist, communist, or socialist space. They form a key part of the left and any leftist coalition. They'll probably always lead most education and organizing efforts. But there's a deeper pool of leftists and potential leftists. Any framework isolating the left to the explicitly anti-capitalist space fails to capture that pool. And any framework opening the left to all or most Democrats fails to capture it for a different reason. Our political terms are unsettled, and our best route is to combine analytical clarity and rigor with openness. For the left, all this stands out as an opportunity for education and solidarity. It means directing political education, outreach, and organizing efforts at the kind of cross-racial, young, working-class coalition targeted by, for example, organizations like Make the Road New York[24] and the 2020 Bernie Sanders presidential campaign.

To provide readers with a ready-made map for drawing these distinctions – both for purposes of reading this book and having discussions with fellow leftists – I've included a table to get at the key differences between liberals, progressives, social democrats, and (democratic) socialists. See Table 1.1 below.

Table 1.1

	Liberal	Progressive	Social Democrat	(Democratic) Socialist
Capitalist System	Support	Support	Support/Mixed	Oppose
Universal Programs	Skeptical	Skeptical	Support as Endpoint	Support as Means to Socialist Ends
Means-Testing	Support	Support	Oppose	Oppose
Government Regulation	Support/Mixed	Support as Endpoint	Support as Endpoint	Support as Means to Socialist Ends
International Solidarity	Oppose	Mixed/Indifferent	Mixed/Indifferent	Support
Bipartisan Consensus	Support	Support	Mixed	Oppose
Example US Politicians	John Kerry, Hillary Clinton	Elizabeth Warren	Bernie Sanders, AOC	???

---

[24] https://maketheroadny.org/. Last accessed July 27, 2020.

In terms of general attitudes toward capitalism and regulation, only socialists oppose capitalism. Liberals support capitalism in something a lot like its present form, while progressives and social democrats want to use regulations and social programs to create a less harmful version of capitalism. Liberals and progressives often favor social programs run by the government, but they want means-tested programs narrowly tailored and targeted toward specific groups of people. Social democrats and socialists, by contrast, prefer universal social programs where the government provides everyone – regardless of their gender, race, socioeconomic status, et al. – with basic necessities like food, health care, housing, and internet access. Socialists add one feature that goes beyond what social democrats prefer – they want to structure universal programs to build toward the expansion of economic democracy beyond necessities and into *all* aspects of the economy. They want workers to own and manage their workplaces.

With regard to foreign policy, liberals and progressives fully support the bipartisan foreign policy consensus that promotes U.S. domination of the world. We'll discuss the bipartisan foreign policy consensus in more detail in Chapter 2. For now, while progressives sometimes show signs of dissent – though they rarely do much with it in practice – liberals practically *never* deviate from the norm on foreign policy. And only socialists regularly promote international solidarity between working-class people as a key part of their foreign policy outlook. For liberals, progressives, and social democrats, international solidarity either directly conflicts with their political aims – liberals and progressives – or are largely irrelevant to their aims – social democrats.

It's important to keep in mind that a table like this one is highly schematic. People and organizations don't always fit into one box at all times. There's also a great deal of movement between groups over time. Even among the politicians I listed as representative examples, we find drift. Had they won the 2004 or 2016 election, respectively, John Kerry and Hillary Clinton likely would've drifted politically to the right and ended up as moderate Democrats rather than liberals. See, for example, the presidency of Barack Obama, who campaigned as a liberal-to-progressive but governed as a moderate. Clinton and Kerry also campaigned as liberals bordering on progressives. Elizabeth Warren has spent most of her political career in the progressive camp, but some of her views are more liberal than progressive. On the other hand, she even dipped at times into the social democratic camp during her 2020 campaign, such as during her brief flirtation with supporting Medicare for All. And while Bernie Sanders is mostly a social democrat, he occasionally dips into socialist territory to the left or progressive territory to the right, depending on the topic. The lack of example of a nationally-known socialist politician in the U.S. also stands out in the table. In the long-term, that's something the left will want to fix.

What's true for individuals is also true for organizations. The Green Party in the U.S. has historically moved back and forth between the progressive and social democrat camps. Prior to 2012, it operated firmly in these realms. Jill Stein, its candidate in 2012 and 2016, then ran multiple social democratic campaigns. However, in 2020, the Green Party jointly ran Howie Hawkins with the Socialist Party USA. This pushed the Green Party rather firmly into the socialist camp. The DSA in the U.S., a major beneficiary (and supporter) of the 2016 Bernie Sanders campaign, built itself in the 1980s from some of the more moderate elements of the old Socialist Party of America. Its outlook was similar to that of the Green Party until the mid-2010s, namely toggling between progressive and social democrat with only the occasional and vague reference to socialism. This changed beginning in 2016 and 2017, as newer, younger leftists joined the organization in droves and pushed it toward the socialist camp. The DSA still retains progressive and social democratic elements, but it's now primarily a socialist organization.

And so, we should use a table like this one as a starting point, as an analytical tool rather than a rigid model. It's a useful tool for gauging views and taking a general approach. But it's not a useful tool for cramming anyone's views into narrow boxes. It's a starting point rather than an end point.

Foreign Policy

With foreign policy, we begin with the question of how much expertise and terminology we really need as leftists looking to organize people. Do we need a bachelor- or graduate-level education in international relations to discuss foreign policy with potential members and voters? Though it might terrify experts and scholars to say so, we *don't* need an expert level understanding of history and jargon. That level of understanding isn't needed for mass movement members or organizers. For one, it's not practical to expect most members of leftist movements – or even most organizers – to achieve it. It requires far more free time and degrees than we're able to put together. But it's also far less important than we might suspect. As leftists building a movement, we're looking to develop popular, democratic power. We can help each person in leftist movements learn enough to engage with basic principles and judge broad matters of public policy. And the entire U.S. left can get to that point. Readers can learn enough about foreign policy schools of thought to follow debates.

The point applies to most political issues. Citizens judge policy, make decisions, vote, and so on, without the kind of deep expertise scholars with graduate degrees hold. The left remains committed to *trusting* people, trusting their judgment. It wants participatory democracy, putting real decision-making power in people's hand without expecting them to be wonks. One key difference between leftists and many liberals and progressives is that leftists believe deeply in democratic, popular power. As organizers, we provide people with the tools they need to live up to these ideals, and we don't do so by holding graduate seminars. I'm offering the following discussion of foreign policy terms and schools with this spirit in mind. I'll provide enough for novice readers and new leftists to find their way around debates. Readers already familiar with basic foreign policy terms and schools may want to skim the rest of the chapter before moving on to Chapter 2.

There's also the question of the scope of foreign policy, particularly what it includes and how it differs from domestic policy. In fact, there's no hard separation between domestic and foreign policy[25]. But we can draw certain tentative boundaries. First and foremost, U.S. foreign policy is about the relationships between the U.S. and the rest of the world. Issues of war and peace might come to readers' minds first, and that's a good start. I'll focus on those issues in much of Part II. But it also includes issues like: foreign aid and military aid, humanitarian work, world government, organizations like the United Nations (UN), international non-governmental organizations (NGOs), the global economy, trade agreements, and many other issues. I'll touch on each where we need to do so. But the U.S. military's use of force will remain my primary focus.

New leftists often think about foreign policy in moral terms, often individual morals. Politicians do the same thing. They think about the U.S. as a person and foreign policy decisions as a collection of individual moral decisions. For example, many people ask questions like, 'should *we* – i.e., the U.S. – invade Iraq?' Politicians and think tanks also make decisions and conduct research with this framing in mind. This framing is a bad one, and later we'll see why, but I want readers to set this issue aside for the moment. The point for now is that foreign policy theories – and the political discussions based on these theories – move beyond individual morality. They get at principles deeper than those captured by individual moral decisions or theories.

We can divide foreign policy thought at a very broad level into realist and liberal theories of international relations among nations. On the realist view, each nation *does* in fact behave very much like an individual, at least according to a certain understanding of the rational person. According to the realist view, each nation pursues its self-interest, with survival as the driving force. The nation, then, operates like a person trying to access and keep resources for their own benefit. On most

---

[25] Arparna Gopalan takes this point even further, arguing that we may want to simply jettison talk of 'foreign policy,' as such. The thought here is that foreign policy specialists focus intently on issues of war and peace and international relations to such an extent that they lose track of how these issues connect both to domestic issues and the operations of international capital. I agree with Gopalan's critique – indeed, my very first principle in the following chapter is one of international solidarity. But I do think the label 'foreign policy' remains worthwhile to pick out particular parts of the larger whole for closer analysis. See Gopalan 2020.

versions of realism, this means the nation is rather competitive and even selfish. Motivated by its own survival and benefit, it consolidates and expands its grip on power. Readers might hear this and assume realists believe nations constantly make war with each other. As it turns out, that's not necessarily true. There are many ways for nations to pursue their self-interest, and war is only one of them. It's often not even the best way to do so. The nation might build power through diplomacy or cooperation with its neighbors. If we lived in a world where no single nation was dominant, a collection of nations could – in theory – maintain a stable peace through cooperation or uneasy tension.

And so, realism turns out to be rather complex. We might bring out this complexity by considering the foreign policy of Richard Nixon, who was very much a realist. He saw a world divided between individual nations pursuing their self-interest. But he thought the U.S. could best achieve its self-interest within an international order balancing power between several key nations. And when we start from this frame, his foreign policy decisions make much more sense. Nixon de-escalated U.S. relations with China, and he gradually turned the Vietnam War over to Vietnamese forces. He passed along fewer wars to the next president than he inherited from Lyndon B. Johnson, his Democratic predecessor. He did so because of the global political environment, an environment where the Soviet Union – among other forces – represented a balancing power to the U.S.

Liberal theories argue in favor of the pursuit of liberal interests and policy objectives, regardless of theories about the rational person and their implications for the behavior of nations. Liberal theorists get rid of the assumption that the nation is like an individual person pursuing their self-interest. In doing so, they open the door to issues beyond those of power and security. For this reason, they often focus on issues like international trade, international order, and organizations like the UN and the World Trade Organization (WTO). Whereas realists often remain skeptical of international order, liberals mostly think one is possible, even desirable. But this is very broad, and different liberal theorists deeply disagree with one another on other matters. Liberal theories run from optimistic and internationally engaged to *extremely* belligerent and empire-building.

Why? They often disagree amongst themselves on the kind of international order that's preferable. In the Fourteen Points speech I cited above, Woodrow Wilson advocated a liberal international order based on a (somewhat) anti-colonial message and the (mostly) peaceful spread of the U.S. system of government around the globe. At the other end of the spectrum, some liberal internationalists want the U.S. to conquer much of the world and spread its system of government by force or other forms of domination. George W. Bush's wars in Afghanistan and Iraq, for example, arguably relied on the same reasoning used by liberal internationalists.

I'll finish this section with two notes. First, realism and liberalism do not exhaust all foreign policy perspectives, nor do they even come close. However, the terms do capture most debates in the U.S. press and scholarly literature. Readers with a solid overview of realism and liberalism can follow and interpret most of those debates. That's why it's important to keep them in mind. Other perspectives – like constructivist, feminist, and post-structural perspectives – raise important concerns with dominant theories, and they provide compelling alternative visions. They helpfully criticize some of the key assumptions I outlined above. And so, many other foreign policy perspectives don't cleanly fit into the realism/liberalism dichotomy. Marxists also bring a number of key points to the table, ones *especially* important for the left. They often argue the entire 'realism' and 'liberalism' dichotomy is a bit of a distraction. Rather, they think foreign policy is grounded in the accumulation of capital and also strongly suspect foreign policy *theory* is influenced by global capital.

Second, we can sketch out another division. This is one between theories about the way the world *currently* works and the way it *should* work. Even the more advanced forms of realism and liberalism often gloss over this distinction. For example, it's possible to be a realist about how the world currently works while also pushing for nations to *change* the way they operate. Perhaps some readers think nations currently operate as self-interested actors but *should* spend more time working through the UN. Some versions of realism allow for this distinction. By contrast, others – ones locating the theory in human nature itself – don't. We can make an analogous point with respect to liberal internationalist theories.

Finally, to be clear at the outset, I'm not advocating in this book for any specific foreign policy theory. For the reasons I outlined at the beginning of this section, I think it's unnecessary. But leftists need to survey the landscape well enough to navigate conversations and make decisions. This means we need to do well enough to, for example, participate in conversations like the one I had at the Iowa caucus. And leftists might need yet again a deeper understanding later when fleshing out more detailed policy. In particular, in-depth policy conversations require a closer study of anti-colonial, feminist, and Marxist perspectives.

A Note on Just War Theory

While not advocating for any particular theory, I'll strongly advocate for an anti-interventionist approach to foreign policy. It will be one of our four basic principles in the next chapter. 'Just war theory' looms large over these debates. And so, I'll offer a brief word on just war theory. This theory frames much of the recent discussion among academics – especially academics at military colleges and universities. And it's roughly what the title suggests: just war theorists debate the criteria for when it's justified to go to war. But to do so requires certain starting assumptions. Almost all just war theorists, for example, think war is justified in *some* circumstances, and most think it's justified in *many* circumstances. Few are *total* pacifists, and most advocate some kind of broad interventionism. They want to figure out what kinds of interventions are good, and what kinds help create a better world. If one thinks intervention is rarely – if ever – justified, then just war theory looks much less compelling as a topic of study.

However, just war theory has never been a large part of the debate on the U.S. left. As a result, I've decided to largely set it aside. The reasons most leftists avoid it are complicated. For one, few leftists teach at military colleges, and few leftists engage with professional military ethics. But that's not a great reason to set just war theory aside, because those debates might offer important perspectives we're ignoring. A second – and better – reason is that just war theorists tend to adopt bad assumptions. They focus on leaders and their decisions, assuming leaders and nations have wide latitude to decide when to go to war. They typically set aside economic factors and global capital. And almost all just war theorists think just wars are *possible*, both theoretically and practically. Many leftists reject some or all of these assumptions, and I think they have strong reasons to do so. One major reason I'll offer to adopt an anti-interventionist approach is that just wars probably *aren't* possible now except in rare circumstances. And so, engaging with just war theory probably isn't productive for the U.S. left.

There's one major exception to all this, and it's one I'll mark at the outset. I'll discuss Michael Walzer's work at various points in this book. He's a leftist and a major just war theorist. His 1977 book *Just and Unjust Wars*[26] is a classic of both just war theory and left foreign policy. Among other engagements with Walzer's work, I'll argue that he takes too strong an interventionist stance. I'll leave open to readers the question of whether this is due to his appeal to just war theory. Interested readers should consult the 1977 book, and they should also consult exchanges between Walzer and Noam Chomsky on just war theory[27].

Despite not focusing on just war theory in particular, we will spend at least some time addressing the general question of when the U.S. should go to war. I see this as a much more practical discussion, and it's one potential leftists want to address. This isn't a question of when an *idealized* nation-state should go to war. Rather, it's a question of when a particular nation-state – the United States – with a particular level of power and relationship to the world – a powerful hegemon, as we'll see in the next chapter – should go to war. While these questions may seem similar, they're not. We'll look specifically at the case of Afghanistan in more depth in the conclusion of the book. But, for now, consider the possibility that an ideal nation-state, devoid of the contexts of hegemony and imperialism, might have been justified to invade Afghanistan in 2001 on grounds of bringing terrorists to justice or replacing a government that oppresses its population. However, a powerful nation-state – a hegemon or imperialist power – might not be justified to invade Afghanistan on the

---

[26] Walzer 2015 [1977].

[27] For Chomsky's side of this discussion, I'd recommend his speech at the U.S. Military Academy called Just War Theory (https://chomsky.info/20060420/) and his article A Just War? Hardly (https://chomsky.info/20060509/). Both last accessed May 30, 2020.

grounds that it can't address the situation in a fair way and can't invade without increasing its own power, much to the detriment of many other nations.

In this chapter, we've learned who makes up the current and potential leftist coalition. And we've gained a grasp of basic foreign policy terms and schools. Let's move on to consider the basic principles of a left foreign policy.

Chapter 2

Basic Principles for a Left Foreign Policy

We began by acknowledging that the left lacks a foreign policy consensus, and then we recognized that a lack of organizing prevents us from reaching that consensus and using it to build more sustained leftist movements. But the left faces even larger short-term challenges. It lacks not only a foreign policy consensus but also the basic building blocks and tools for creating one. The left doesn't yet have the materials to do so. Furthermore, as leftists we stand at a loss for how to get started. The good news is that we can solve these problems. In this chapter, I'll propose building blocks to get us started, building blocks that will serve us well for many years to come. And then I'll move on to the concrete issue of open borders in the next chapter and U.S. relations with specific countries in Part II.

The building blocks I propose come in the form of four basic principles: international solidarity, anti-interventionism, pluralism, and fighting global capital. These principles form the materials from which we will build a foreign policy. That's, of course, a very straight reading of the building blocks metaphor: we arrive at basic principles, and then we apply those principles to new events through detailed, developed policies and strategies. In this way, our building blocks constitute our materials for the job. Of course, moving from these basic principles to a foreign policy consensus will take time and work. Furthermore, we'll need careful, democratic deliberation and decision-making as a part of our toolkit. But done well, we'll draw in new members and build fruitful connections with comrades throughout the world. The process of moving from consensus to detailed, developed policy and strategies is yet another step, though it's one that can rely on – and build upon – the expertise gained from earlier steps. This latter part comes much later, and I'll set it aside for now.

At the same time, building blocks aren't *just* materials for the job, just as any material isn't simply some inert object. The materials we use shape both the process and the product. They hint at, suggest, and push us toward particular ways of building. They show us the way toward progress and prevent us from building something that collapses. Take cooking as an example. If we're making an apple pie, we use a set of ingredients including apple, sugar, flour, butter, and spices, among other things. Simple enough. But we have choices: sweet or tart apples, organic or non-organic butter, different flours for the crust, different spices, different baking agents, et al. We can make the crust by hand and cut the apples with knives, or we can use dough hooks, pastry blenders, or mechanical slicers. These choices impact consistency and taste, and our choices at one step push us in different directions in the following steps. Foreign policy works much the same way. The principles themselves will suggest whether we should adopt democratic or less democratic methods, broad and open or narrow and specialized policies, total commitment to peaceful methods or openness to war in some circumstances, and so on.

Analytical clarity at the outset is crucial to coming to the right decisions. And so, I'll start here with a couple of basic questions: First, what makes a foreign policy 'leftist,' and to what does 'leftist' stand opposed? Second, what foreign policy views predominate today, and how should ours contrast to those? Answering these questions provides us with key guidance.

Leftist Foreign Policy

The answer to the first question harkens back to our discussion of 'left' and 'leftist' from the previous chapter. We know that at a minimum, the left stands against the capitalist system and in favor of replacing capitalism with a democratic system of ownership and control over the economy. Most leftists think about these things along the lines of domestic policy. After all, what is democratic control and ownership of the economy if not democracy within the *workplace?* Applications to foreign policy are far less clear[28]. What do issues of war and peace, in particular, have to do with any of *that*, anyway? Leftists start to flounder around this sort of question. They hold an initial opposition to war – a reaction against it, because it's bad for people. It's less clear how to connect these anti-war concerns with the kinds of domestic issues they're worried about. This is the more philosophical component to why leftists have a tough time holding conversations like the ones I had at the Iowa caucus.

Our starting point, then, is a point of contrast. Leftist foreign policy stands outside of and against capitalism. The first challenge lies in determining what's going on *inside* – how our current U.S. foreign policy actively *supports* capital, especially via the use of military force. Answering the analytical questions involved here often separates good from bad leftist practice. We have plenty of examples of both – from the highly beneficial and fruitful black international solidarity movement with Cuba in the 1890s and Ghana in the 1950s and 1960s to Bayard Rustin's embarrassing failure to oppose the Vietnam War[29]. The left needs good answers to these analytical questions to make sure it's arriving at the right decisions. It needs to understand dominant approaches to U.S. foreign policy, in particular the bipartisan foreign policy consensus that has dominated foreign policy for decades. It needs this in order to show how the interests of U.S. elites and global capital run the show. A leftist consensus will be one that stands against this dominant approach and in favor of anti-capitalist alternatives.

Some of this is all too familiar to veterans of foreign policy debates and grassroots activism. But for many people newer to leftist movements – whether they currently identify as liberal, progressive, or even democratic socialist – this is new and unfamiliar terrain. Readers in this camp might

---

[28] See Gopalan 2020 for discussion of this point. Gopalan argues that the apparent disconnect between domestic and foreign policy issues is so severe that we should largely shun discussion of foreign policy in favor of discussion of global solidarity.

[29] Steve Striffler discusses both of these cases in Striffler 2019. Jacobin also covers in more depth the regression of Rustin's career from support for broad, leftist coalitions to failure to integrate foreign policy into his vision. See: https://jacobinmag.com/2018/05/the-tragedy-of-bayard-rustin/. Last accessed July 28, 2020.

not yet draw the right connections between what the U.S. does overseas and what it does at home. Even if they do, they might lack awareness of the close links between U.S. foreign policy and global capital – even the foreign policy stances adopted by liberal and progressive politicians they admire and vote for. Foreign policy issues are shockingly bipartisan, and we won't create a left foreign policy by 'voting blue no matter who' and hoping for the best. Nor will we create one by advocating for 'progressivism' as an umbrella label or program. Even politicians and political movements quite favorable to the left on issues of domestic policy – from Ayanna Pressley and Elizabeth Warren to the Working Families Party – remain silent about foreign policy or stake out ground not much different from that of generic Democrats or even generic Republicans.

And so, it's important to understand at the outset that the existing political system is utterly *disordered* on foreign policy. The contrast between a left foreign policy and mainstream U.S. foreign policy is not a matter of degree or the pace at which we make progress. From right-wing Republicans to progressive Democrats, the entire mainstream spectrum shares in the disorder. What we need is a complete, radical transformation of the foreign policy landscape. Here we find a contrast to domestic policy. On domestic policy, we find differences of degree among moderates, liberals, progressives, and sometimes even social democrats or democratic socialists. Barack Obama wanted to raise the minimum wage to $10.10 while progressives and social democrats want to raise it to $15. Perhaps some democratic socialists want to raise it to $20 or even $25. But they all want to raise it. While there might be underlying differences of political philosophy, the policy implications amount to details under the same broad theme. Foreign policy rarely works this way. In foreign policy, the vast majority of the political system wants to continue U.S. foreign and military aid and/or military occupations. The left wants to end those occupations. The political system wants to create a trade system that undermines the power of nations to implement pro-worker policies. The left wants a worker-centered trade system. These differences admit of little room for compromise, and switching from one team to the other is more like a conversion experience than a move along a scale.

The left needs and wants to organize grassroots movements. To do so, it needs organizers who understand the vast chasm between a foreign policy built on leftist principles and the one that currently drives U.S. policy. It needs a rank-and-file that can discuss these differences with family, friends, and well-meaning strangers like the woman I met at the Iowa caucuses. The scope of these differences presents both challenges and opportunities. On the one hand, the left position might seem pie-in-the-sky or utopian. But many people find it appealing, even people one might not normally think of as leftists or as participants in leftist movements. It coheres nicely with the moral intuitions of many Americans – what they think the country should ideally do. Few people *really* want to be on the side of death and destruction. It's up to the left to show in detail how that's exactly where current U.S. foreign policy leads. The left vision might be ambitious and remote from current politics, but it's one we can defend – both on the merits and on the basis of intuitions most Americans share.

The Bipartisan Foreign Policy Consensus and Leftists

This leaves us with the task of sorting out the currently dominant foreign policy views in order to shed light on alternatives. To do so, we'll analyze the bipartisan foreign policy consensus and the alternatives leftists already offer. There are certain military interventions in U.S. history – notably World War II and the 2001 War in Afghanistan – that the entire mainstream U.S. political spectrum supports. Even many leftists support *these* interventions. And so, it appears we have a fruitful starting point for sorting out basic principles. We might ask what these areas of agreement have in common and where the left should situate itself. But in fact, it's far murkier than this. Any move beyond these kinds of cases reveals spirited debate and entrenched disagreement. This holds even within the most mainstream, 'establishment' of political spaces. From the Vietnam War to the 1991 Gulf War to more recent conflicts in Iraq and Syria, supporters and opponents within both political parties debated throughout the country. In some of these conflicts, victory for the pro-war side was hardly assured until the votes had been cast or the decisions made.

And there's the rub. At the level of policy details, the bipartisan foreign policy 'consensus' doesn't look like much of a consensus at all! It admits of disagreement on action and methods. In the previous chapter, we looked at different philosophical approaches to foreign policy – realism and liberal internationalism. Calling it all a consensus attributes to it a uniformity it neither achieves nor even aspires to. Nevertheless, there *is* a consensus here. We find it at a deeper level. Regardless of whether conservative or liberal politicians – or realist or liberal experts – support a particular intervention, a deeper vision unites them. They're all committed to maintaining the perceived status and interests of the U.S. in its international relations. And they want to do so through political and military enforcement of some kind. The U.S. maintains a world economic and political system that serves its own interests. And it holds many tools to do so: international institutions, military strength, and military and humanitarian aid to other nations, among others.

One might ask the natural question: if U.S. politicians agree on a foreign policy *vision*, why do they disagree so often on *policy*? As it turns out, it's not always clear what U.S. interests are and how to best serve them. When Barack Obama and Republicans argued in the 2010s about whether to conduct airstrikes in Syria, they disagreed on whether airstrikes were good for U.S. interests. Were they the right way to maintain the U.S.'s position in the Middle East and therefore its advantages in the world's economic and political system? Neither side argued that the political situation in the Middle East *shouldn't* serve U.S. interests. Both sides accepted U.S. dominance as a matter of course. All sides in U.S. politics share a commitment to U.S. interests and also – paradoxically, as we'll see – to the view that the U.S. acts with the best of intentions in its international engagements.

Here we find our first point of contrast between the left and mainstream U.S. politics, from conservative to progressive. The left doesn't put U.S. interests – whether perceived or actual – over and above broader, international interests. And leftists are quite skeptical about the so-called 'good intentions' of the U.S. in its international engagements. The left wants a better world for *everyone*, a world serving our collective interests across international borders. This is a world without U.S. dominance –

whether 'enlightened' or not. It's a world where people work together across borders to achieve those interests rather than compete with one another for scarce resources. As leftists, we don't take this stance for reasons of self-flagellation or self-sacrifice. Our goal is not to lower our own standard of living or that of the rest of the U.S. Rather, our goal is to put together a vision for a larger, more inclusive world where everyone can grow sustainably together.

I think most leftists understand this in the abstract. And we consistently oppose the most visible manifestations of U.S. dominance, like the 2003 War in Iraq. The key problem is that we're often bad at opposing less obvious manifestations of U.S. dominance. We rarely develop our understanding comprehensively or apply it beyond the most obvious cases. To take these next steps, we need to move from the abstract to the more concrete. Let's think about how this all plays out in more difficult cases.

Empire vs. Hegemony

I turned 18 years old shortly before 9/11, just as I was beginning to become involved in leftist movements. This marked a major transition point in both my life and in the U.S. left. In the 1990s, the U.S. left honed in on globalized trade. Its most important tools were the corporate campaign and the anti-globalization demonstration[30]. In the wake of 9/11, the left quickly turned to issues of war and peace. Some of the tools remained the same, particularly the public demonstration. While opposition to something we called 'U.S. imperialism' was central to our anti-war work, we shifted focus too quickly. As a result, we never developed a deeper understanding of how these forces of imperialism work. Nor did we effectively use the work already done among our own ranks, especially by anti-colonial and anti-imperialist groups. The left agreed on little other than a half-baked framework wherein the U.S. was an empire hell-bent on expansion. Aside from slogans – 'no blood for oil,'

---

[30] Corporate campaigns typically involve focused action and boycotts against particular companies and/or industries. The idea is to put economic pressure on companies to discontinue unfair labor practices. The anti-sweatshop movement, in particular, put the corporate campaign to widespread use. Striffler 2019 provides a historical overview of the corporate campaign in Ch. 6.

for example – we didn't know *why* the U.S. wanted expansion. Just that it did.

The left's approach to the wars in Afghanistan and Iraq – opposition to U.S. imperialism – suffered from the same problems as our approach to the bipartisan foreign policy consensus. Namely, it glossed over the complex perspectives and voices within even establishment politics. It's not that the left totally missed the mark. Empire has long been an important way the U.S. achieves its foreign policy goals. There's even a standard narrative around this: the U.S. staked out bold opposition to European colonialism in the early 19th century with the Monroe Doctrine. While the U.S. originally formulated the Monroe Doctrine as a warning against European empires in the Western Hemisphere, it next turned that doctrine into an excuse to wage war up and down the Hemisphere and later around the globe. This process began with the expansion of the U.S. across the territory that would become the continental United States. It continued through U.S. intervention against the Spanish Empire in Cuba, resulting in U.S. military rule of Cuba and eventual full annexation of Guantanamo Bay. And the U.S. extended this by annexing the Philippines from Spain. By the early 20th century, the U.S. ruled a globe-spanning empire of its own.

But the left underestimated the complexity of these events in multiple ways. In the anti-war movements of the early 2000s, many leftists treated Afghanistan and Iraq as unique cases. They missed the connections with a long imperial tradition, and they left this tradition out of their diagnoses of the cases. For too many leftists, each generation reinvents its basic theory of an expansionist U.S. empire, ignorant of the deep imperial policy roots. Perhaps more importantly, many leftists fail to notice shifts over time in the focus of U.S. imperial policy. While the U.S. still pursues expansionism and direct rule in select cases, it more often operates through more subtle forms of control and domination. Expansionist empire is only one way the U.S. dominates the world, and it's often not the most important way. We need a distinction between U.S. imperialism in the late 19th and early 20th centuries on the one hand and U.S. imperialism after World War II on the other[31].

Daniel Immerwahr addressed both of these points in his recent book, *How to Hide an Empire*[32]. Immerwahr argues that politicians, the media, and educators erased much of this imperial phase from our collective U.S. history – our history as Americans and even as leftists. Thus, many Americans – again, even leftists – remain ignorant about the history of U.S. empire. Certainly *some* leftists know the history and impact of imperial policy, often leftists who are the victims of that policy. Native American groups, in particular, live with knowledge of the impact of U.S. empire. Many black Americans live with knowledge of the domestic systems the U.S. put in place to support its empire, knowledge gained from bearing the brunt of decades of racist policy. But many leftists lack access to this knowledge as a result of the way these institutions operate. Revealing and spreading that knowledge is a key part of good leftist practice.

On the second point, Immerwahr argues that U.S. foreign policy took a major turn at the end of World War II in the context of the Cold War. Particularly in the 1950s and 1960s, the U.S. heavily adopted anti-Soviet and pro-liberation rhetoric. It portrayed the Soviet Union as a hostile, imperialistic conqueror, particularly in eastern Europe. In turn, the Soviet Union portrayed the U.S. as a racist, colonialist state, particularly in the Jim Crow south. The U.S. needed a foreign policy that bolstered its position with respect to the Soviets. It found such a policy by dominating the world through the use of international institutions and rules. In short, yesterday's U.S. empire met today's anti-colonial movement, with the U.S. pivoting in response to a subtler Soviet threat. Immerwahr argues this is a major break from previous U.S. foreign policy because it's less ham-fisted and more difficult to resist. Among other reasons, it has no obvious target for resistance – no soldier in the street, governor in the mansion, et

---

[31] There's another period of U.S. imperialism in addition to these two, and it's the one from before the late 19th century. As Vine 2020 points out, the U.S. began its wars of expansion from the very moment of its founding in the late 18th century.
[32] Immerwahr 2019.

al. How can the left fight an empire devoid of the most obvious markers of empire?

The newer strategy is one of hegemony, a strategy of subtle domination through institutions and rules[33]. Its best examples are international institutions like the United Nations and UN Security Council. But it manifests itself in various functions. Its judicial functions include the international criminal courts. Its finance and trade functions include the World Bank, World Trade Organization, and International Monetary Fund. This hegemonic domination is deeper and more effective than we often realize on the left. Much of the reason is that it's easy to pass off as impartial and objective. Putting U.S. soldiers in the street and a U.S.-appointed governor in the capitol building creates obvious symbols and targets for resistance. But international institutions appear to have legitimacy, seeming to work for the interests of the people being dominated. Resisting these institutions requires different strategies, and anti-colonial movements work hard at doing so.

One of Immerwahr's more compelling examples of hegemonic domination is an extended discussion of standards and measurements. He discusses these through organizations like the International Standards Organization[34] (ISO). The ISO standardizes products and measurements to facilitate world trade. Historically, different parts of the world made products and tools that were incompatible with one another. For one example – as many of us know – the U.S. is a rare holdout from the international metric system of measurement. It's able to do this – and able to force other countries to comply – by using its extensive power. It maintains its power in part through – among other things – forcing the world to comply with its idiosyncratic system of measurement! And so,

---

[33] The distinction between empire and hegemony is a controversial one in many leftist circles. Many authors simply choose to put the two together under the heading of 'imperialism,' taking more subtle hegemonic strategies to be simply part of an imperial program. See, for example, Veltmeyer and Petras 2014 for an example of this strategy. For Veltmeyer and Petras, subtle forms of domination by corporations and even nonprofits and NGOs are simply extensions of imperial policy. In a sense, they're right. They're certainly extensions of policies that serve U.S. interests. But to put them together papers over real differences in how the U.S. achieves policy and the ways we need to talk with new leftists about U.S. policy.

[34] This is sometimes written as the International Organization for Standardization.

international standards appear benign and objective, but they're *not*. Nations spend untold amounts of effort and money reconfiguring their infrastructure to meet the needs of the United States. What sounds boring and innocent was in fact a major problem for some parts of the world.

But while Immerwahr is correct to point to a shift from classical imperial policy to hegemonic policy, the shift is incomplete. Empire remains very much a live and widely accepted option in the U.S. foreign policy toolkit. Furthermore, the U.S. and other empires always aspired to hegemony of some kind or another. In a review of Immerwahr's book in *Catalyst*[35], Christian Appy points out limits to the broad narrative frame of empire-to-hegemony. The narrative papers over many of the ways U.S. empire – and U.S. imperial policy – still exist even in a hegemonic era. While there might have been a shift from empire to hegemony, empire always lurks in the background. In at least some sense, this should be an obvious point for the left. The very policies motivating many young leftist activists – like the War in Iraq – demonstrate Appy's point well. Appy teaches us, though, not to get too lost in subtlety[36].

Empire and hegemony are seemingly very different approaches to foreign policy. They certainly have different outcomes and require different resistance tactics. But the U.S. has used both for a long time. And the approaches share in an underlying sameness – the commitment to maintaining the U.S.'s dominant position and serving its perceived interests. A critique that hits U.S. imperialism alone is unlikely to address the less visible ways the U.S. exerts power. But a critique that hits only U.S. hegemony is unlikely to emphasize and forcefully oppose the ways the U.S. uses military power, even in so-called 'humanitarian interventions.' The left must address both approaches[37].

---

[35] Appy 2019.

[36] It's worth noting the converse – that more subtle U.S. policy involving operating through client states, et al., rather than directly occupying foreign powers – was also part of the U.S. foreign policy toolkit before World War II. See Vine 2020 for extensive examples of this. And so, it's best to read Immerwahr as making a point about the relative prevalence of these types of policies before and after World War II.

[37] It's also worth asking about the systems and infrastructure that enable the U.S. to carry out its more recent policy moves. We'll look at this in more depth in Part II. But, for now, it's worth

Principles for a Left Foreign Policy

As the left's domestic policy looks toward *domestic* social democracy in the short-term, its foreign policy must look toward *international* social democracy in the short-term. As leftists, we must look toward a united, cross-border strategy. But social democratic movements – not only in the U.S., but throughout the world – are traditionally *national*, not *international*. This is a major challenge. Nations like Norway and Sweden took great strides toward social democracy in the 20th century. They used the levers of state power to provide to their own citizens many of the benefits the left wants for people in the U.S. But these benefits rested in part on economic forces harmful to working-class people *elsewhere*. Norway paid for its own social democracy with oil revenues dependent on exploitation of workers and damage to the environment[38]. Sweden has long been a major exporter of military weaponry[39]. The U.S. left can't benefit at the expense of others because this doesn't advance the fight against global capital. We can't create social democracy at home by enabling the forces that will ultimately undo social democracy at home.

As Tejasvi Nagaraja points out in an essay on leftist foreign policy[40], our domestic movements stand in key relations to international movements. The Movement for Black Lives, in particular, stresses the link from divestment from wars and international military aid to investment in domestic programs[41]. Our challenge is to craft a left foreign policy where nations rise together. Our building blocks – the four basic principles – will guide us. Creating social democracy in one nation often depends on

---

pointing again to Vine 2020. Vine lays out a compelling case for the particular importance of military bases to the U.S.'s policy of not directly governing its client states.

[38] Norway's social democracy dates to the years of Einar Gerharsen's time as prime minister, which pre-dates its discovery of oil. But oil played a large role in sustaining that social democracy. For one take on Norwegian social democracy from an outsider, see Joplin 2020.

[39] See, among other potential examples, Radio Sweden's coverage at: https://sverigesradio.se/sida/artikel.aspx?programid=2054&artikel=4400425. Last accessed: May 26, 2020.

[40] See Nagaraja 2020.

[41] Ibid., pp. 201-202. Nagaraja also points to Rashida Tlaib as a politician who's especially effective at rhetorically linking domestic to international policy.

competition with others. Social democracy succeeds, therefore, by taking advantage of economic circumstances elsewhere. It's rare for nations to succeed by building social democracy *together*. This is a major reason why the left arrived at consensus on domestic policy but not on foreign policy. Finding a way for working-class people across borders to rise together will clear a path toward consensus.

I'll be clear at the outset that this is a *practical* point, not merely a *moral* one. Working together across borders isn't just the right thing to do. It's also the only method that will create sustainable progress. Capital developed tools to fight social democracy in single nations, especially in our current era of financial, globalized capitalism. It has significantly eroded social democracy in Norway and Sweden – among other places – by using these tools. It can and will do the same in the U.S. Thus, we have to lift up our fellow workers in other places to achieve social democracy together. Only by closing capital's windows of opportunity to pit us against one another will we defeat it anywhere. *The four basic principles that will set us on our way are: international solidarity, anti-interventionism, pluralism, and fighting global capital.*

Principle 1: International Solidarity

Our first basic principle – international solidarity – involves working across borders with comrades in other nations on campaigns of human rights, political rights, labor rights, and liberation. This work has two key components. The first is assisting one another in concrete ways, like aiding in fights against political repression and building strike support. We can collect funds, draw attention to local fights, and join one another's battles. The relationship runs both ways, with workers in the U.S. and workers elsewhere providing support as needed. The second is fighting the U.S. government's efforts at aiding the wrong side in these conflicts. There's a great deal of untapped potential of working-class people in the U.S. to stop U.S. efforts to do harm. Put together, international solidarity efforts build awareness, political capacity, and relationships among working-class people around the globe. It provides the substance of class consciousness, creating it from the ground up through shared struggle.

Only through international solidarity will we put in place what we need to work together on the larger project of international social democracy.

While U.S. workers once had a proud tradition of international solidarity, this solidarity is at a historic low point[42]. Furthermore, we've hit this low point at a time of unprecedented global communications and access to information about the rest of the world. This is a mystery, and it's one we have to solve. We can tweet or send a Facebook message to comrades in the Kurdish People's Protection Units (YPG) in Syria in the blink of an eye. But many of us don't know what the YPG is or what it's fighting for[43]. By contrast, U.S. leftists built an international solidarity movement with the Spanish left in the 1930s – and even organized troop shipments – long before the world had the Internet.

What are the conditions – educational, historical, logistical – for developing a robust solidarity movement? Did we have them *then*, and do we lack them *now*? If so, what do we lack – the historical moment or merely the educational background or logistical capacity? Or do we lack *all* of these things? I don't have the answers to all of these questions, but they're the ones we should ask. What I can do is discuss examples of solidarity movements – how they operate, why they succeed, and how they fail. This will provide material for creating new international solidarity movements for a new time.

In his book *Solidarity: Latin America and the US Left in the Era of Human Rights*[44], Steve Striffler reviews the history of leftist international solidarity movements, providing a starting point for the left to recapture this magic. I draw three major conclusions from Striffler's work.

First, he focuses on the types of movements with the greatest chances for success. Successful movements build action around clear visions for collective liberation, and they're centered on the leadership of the people directly impacted. Why do they succeed? They build alliances between members of marginalized groups and the people most familiar with leftist

---

[42] While solidarity is at a low point, there are still solidarity movements. We'll discuss several in later chapters, including black solidarity with Palestine and solidarity campaigns with Venezuela.
[43] 'YPG' designates the People's Protection Units, a group of mostly Kurdish resistance fighters. I'll discuss the YPG in more detail in Part II when discussing Syria.
[44] Striffler 2019.

theory and movement building. Striffler draws attention to this time and again, but a couple of cases stand out. During Cuban anti-slavery campaigns in the mid to late 19th century, black Americans proved to be extremely effective allies to Cubans. Among Americans, they carried the most direct experience with the institution of slavery. Black Americans corralled their experience in anti-slavery movements to mobilize black voters in the Reconstruction Era South. Among other things, they won state government resolutions in favor of Cuban liberation[45]. During the U.S. occupation of the Dominican Republic and Haiti from the 1910s, black Americans – particularly black Americans of Caribbean descent – formed alliances between black civil rights groups like the NAACP, Communist groups, and leftist publications like *The Nation*. Together, they publicly exposed the brutality of these occupations. Their movements expanded from this excellent starting point. Opposition to the occupations eventually reached even the liberal press and Haitian immigrant groups[46].

Second, Striffler focuses on the ideological range of useful collaboration. Left-liberal alliances offer both the most promise and the greatest challenges for successful solidarity movements. The Central American solidarity movement had more participants than any solidarity movements in history. It mobilized tens of thousands of Americans to raise awareness of U.S. military abuses, shine light on the abuses of human rights in El Salvador and other countries, and pledge civil disobedience in the event of a U.S. invasion[47]. It had many successes: providing aid, supporting refugees, and opening space for democratic participation in Nicaragua and El Salvador[48]. On the other hand, the inclusion of liberals – and sometimes even moderates – limited the movement in serious ways. The movement largely set aside the language of collective liberation in favor of the more ambiguous language of 'human rights.' This attracted more people – particularly liberals and moderates – but it pushed the movement away from direct critiques of neoliberal

---

[45] Ibid., pp. 32-33.
[46] Ibid., pp. 50-62.
[47] Ibid., p. 125.
[48] Ibid., pp. 139-140.

capitalism. This limited the scope of El Salvador and Nicaragua solidarity, and it even more strictly limited solidarity with Chile, a nation at the forefront of neoliberal ideology at the time[49]. It also pushed movements to focus on imminent crises and the worst abuses to the exclusion of deeper critique. As a result, movements shifted from one crisis to the next rather than consolidating and building upon gains[50].

Third, Striffler focuses on the weaknesses in solidarity movements preventing them from sustaining themselves and building long-term campaigns for popular power. Ideological divisions and lack of an animating vision are key to these problems. There have been many excellent collaborative efforts between black internationalists and white leftists, particularly in the late 19th and early 20th centuries. But anti-communism drove wedges between these groups after World War II, when mainstream labor largely abandoned leftist solidarity in favor of economic nationalism and the politics of cultural resentment[51]. There's a need to remain ever vigilant against repetition of these problems. For today's left, the challenge is building a strong enough vision – and deep enough relationships through collective struggle – to effectively combat divisions of this kind.

Global capital achieved international solidarity a long time ago. It's deep within the structure of the capitalist system, but globalization in our recent decades of financial capitalism has strengthened these bonds. And so, the left has work to do to build a leftist, internationalist working-class solidarity movement strong enough to win. The best international solidarity movements build collaboration between labor, the left, and members of other oppressed and marginalized groups. And the best way to achieve this collaboration is through connecting people together under a broad umbrella. Efforts will include leftist political education, anti-racist and anti-colonial theory and practice, and direct action and mutual aid. These movements build the kind of collective power needed for the larger battles down the road.

---

[49] Ibid., pp. 116-117.
[50] Ibid., pp. 140-142.
[51] Ibid., p. 150.

Principle 2: Anti-Interventionism

Our second basic principle – anti-interventionism – stands out because it's 'negative' in tone. It's built primarily on *opposing* what the U.S. currently does rather than *building* a leftist alternative. That's intentional. The left has to start from a realization that the current political system cannot yet implement left foreign policy goals. We must recognize the depth of the problems before building a new system. In this sense, fierce opposition to the War in Iraq, for example, was the right move.

The left has made significant progress in the anti-interventionist domain in the last few decades. During the era of economic nationalism and anti-communism after World War II, many leftists supported the Korean War, Vietnam War, and other brazen displays of U.S. imperialism[52]. Anti-interventionist movements rarely extended beyond small, sectarian divisions of the radical peace and/or socialist movements. And when they did, they extended mostly to pro-Soviet groups. By the 21st century, leftists opposed comparable U.S. military interventions. The movement against the war in Iraq reached more people than any anti-war movement in history[53]. Leftists even anticipated and demonstrated against potential *future* action in places like Iran and Syria[54]. It's difficult to overstate this accomplishment.

However, leftist anti-interventionism doesn't yet extend beyond the most visible cases. Nor is it grounded in well understood principles. The

---

[52] See Gallup polling on the Vietnam War: https://news.gallup.com/poll/230558/americans-views-vietnam-war-1960s-trends.aspx. Last accessed: May 26, 2020. As late as 1969, a strong majority of the public still approved of the war, even after the U.S. war effort was widely recognized as unsuccessful.

[53] By contrast to Vietnam, Gallup polling showed a majority of Americans believed the Iraq War was a mistake as early as 2004: https://news.gallup.com/poll/1633/iraq.aspx. Last accessed: May 26, 2020. Also of note is that this general trend holds for domestic issues as well. After the police killing of George Floyd in May 2020, a literal majority of Americans were in favor of burning down a Minneapolis police precinct, according to a Monmouth University poll. See https://www.newsweek.com/54-americans-think-burning-down-minneapolis-police-precinct-was-justified-after-george-floyds-1508452. This is nothing short of astonishing.

[54] As some leftists have pointed out, Joe Biden has signaled hostility to Iran, in particular, in his career and at the start of his administration. See Brownlee 2021. His first major military action in 2021, notably, was against Iran.

left is often much quieter when it comes to economic sanctions or aid without a visible military component, such as sanctions against Libya, North Korea, Russia, or Venezuela. We're not having the far-reaching debates we need to have around U.S. military interventions with allegedly humanitarian goals, like the one in Serbia in the 1990s. These debates are critical because the cumulative impact of these 'small' cases form most of the substance – and likely even most of the impact – of U.S. foreign policy. And while lack of awareness is no doubt part of why the left remains silent in many cases, many leftists still accept the assumption that the U.S. is a well-intentioned actor on the international stage. They think the U.S. *wants* to promote some kind of democratic capitalism via foreign aid and sanctions. It's just that it sometimes makes mistakes along the way. That's wrong, and it shows a misreading of how power works.

In her book *Aiding and Abetting: U.S. Foreign Assistance and State Violence*[55], Jessica Trisko Darden argues that the U.S.'s 'humanitarian' interventions mostly fail. She focuses primarily on non-military foreign aid. It's the sort of stuff almost everyone – even many leftists – believe is helpful at best or benign at worst. However, her research shows a strong association between U.S. foreign aid and state violence in recipient nations. The bigger picture is that the U.S. gives aid to violent political regimes promoting perceived U.S. interests in their region. Despite surface appearances to the contrary, this aid is extremely harmful. And it's harmful even when it doesn't arrive directly in the form of weapons or military training.

Darden points out that foreign aid is highly fungible, meaning that U.S. foreign aid recipients often redirect it to more violent purposes. They can take U.S. food aid and use it for weapons or military training. Even when they're unable to divert the aid itself, they can use it to supplement social spending in order to move *that* money to police or military repression[56]. As an example of this, she provides the case of U.S. aid to Indonesia during its 1975 invasion of East Timor. The U.S. aligned the aid to President

---

[55] Darden 2020.
[56] Ibid., pp. 23-25.

Harry Truman's earlier, lofty-sounding foreign policy vision[57] – seemingly humanitarian goals endorsed by practically the entire mainstream of U.S. politics and foreign policy thought – and so it was hardly an outlier in terms of U.S. policy decisions. The U.S. used the aid as a tactic to prevent Indonesia's President Sukarno from turning pro-Soviet[58]. In reality, the aid provided food support, freeing up later President Suharto to increase his capacity for mass violence[59].

In her study, Darden compares economic aid to military aid. She finds a strong association between U.S. economic aid and both mass killings and state killings in the recipient country. She also finds an association between economic aid and political repression[60]. Perhaps most surprisingly, she finds less association between these things and *military aid*. She speculates this is because military aid tends to encourage the professionalization of militaries[61]. Darden provides El Salvador as a case study of this phenomenon, where U.S. aid to the regime in the 1980s likely prevented it from military and financial collapse. Aid thereby enabled the regime to wage war on popular groups and avoid a political solution to its Civil War[62]. While the U.S. 'accomplished' its anti-Communist goals[63], it did so at the cost of drastically increasing state violence and mass killings. And it left the nation with, at best, a quasi-democratic government with extremely high levels of inequality[64]. For the left, such a trade-off is hardly acceptable.

Finally, Darden points out that these phenomena are not unique to U.S. policy during the Cold War. There's nothing special about the Cold War era leading to ill effects of U.S. aid not replicated in other contexts. Military aid is slightly less harmful since 1990 than it was before then,

---

[57] The 'Truman Doctrine' has been widely discussed in the literature, and the reader might benefit from Wikipedia's overview: https://en.wikipedia.org/wiki/Truman_Doctrine. Last accessed: May 26, 2020.

[58] Darden 2020, pp. 45-46.

[59] Ibid., pp. 54-56.

[60] Ibid., pp. 37-39.

[61] Ibid., pp. 39-41.

[62] Ibid., p. 64.

[63] Ibid., pp. 77-79.

[64] Ibid., p. 66.

perhaps due to better guidelines for providing it or better training for troops in recipient countries[65]. But economic aid still carries the same associations. In fact, it's even *more* strongly associated with mass killing since 9/11 than before 9/11[66]. Well intentioned legislation from foreign policy liberals to limit the negative impact of aid – like laws written by progressive Senators Tom Harkin and Patrick Leahy – have not served their stated function[67]. Darden points to U.S. aid to South Sudan as a recent case where corruption and graft, regulatory failure, and state violence come together[68]. This represents a clear case where the left can put forward an anti-interventionist vision much stronger than that offered by even 'liberals' or 'progressives.'

Darden's work comes from a more conservative and libertarian tradition of anti-interventionism. This is true of much of the current military anti-interventionist tradition in the U.S[69]. This fact makes some leftists nervous. However, I chose to highlight Darden's work here for a key reason. The situation presents the left with potential for unusual and fruitful pragmatic alliances, but it also presents special dangers. We must stick to our leftist principles while remaining open to working on special projects with strange allies. Balancing these forces requires thinking again about the distinction between the 'positive' and 'negative' components of our anti-interventionist principle. The negative component of anti-interventionism is a broad opposition to state intervention. The state in its current form acts in the perceived national interest along the lines of the consensus outlined earlier, and so it's *not* a well-intentioned actor. While the U.S. left understands this in cases like the War in Iraq, it misses

---

[65] Ibid., pp. 100-101.

[66] Ibid., pp. 101-102.

[67] Ibid., pp. 6-8.

[68] Ibid., pp. 103-106.

[69] This is true of both think tanks and individual researchers. Think tanks from this perspective include organizations like the Coalition for a Realistic Foreign Policy and the Quincy Institute for Responsible Statecraft. While different in many respects, these organizations share a commitment to a broadly realist foreign policy orientation and opposition to the building of U.S. Empire. They're much less clear on their attitudes toward U.S. hegemony. On the individual researcher side, readers might consult the work of William Appleman Williams or Andrew Bacevich. Note, in particular Bacevich 2004 and Bacevich 2013.

applications to foreign intervention and aid more broadly. It applies even to many acts of alleged 'humanitarianism.' As leftists, we should broadly oppose intervention. This is the piece of the puzzle where we can work together with some conservatives and libertarians against liberal internationalists.

But there's a positive component, and it's here where we draw a sharp contrast between leftists, on the one hand, and conservative and libertarian anti-interventionists, on the other. Once we've built international solidarity connections and movements, we can work together on direct intervention that works *around* the state rather than *through* it. We can solve problems directly with working-class organizations elsewhere. In the long-term, as the left builds power in the U.S., it can change the conditions under which the U.S. intervenes. As we build movements, win local campaigns for working people and tenants, and eventually win state and national elections, we can create the conditions under which the state intervenes as a force for international social democracy and eventually socialism. Conservatives and libertarians, of course, have no interest in building these forces for positive state intervention.

But we're not there yet. And it's paramount we don't pretend we are. In our current political environment, even Bernie Sanders would run into extreme difficulty taking positive interventions. He would even run into difficulty resisting the subtly negative ones. Other than perhaps Barbara Lee[70], few U.S. politicians consistently oppose intervention. Until we change the underlying conditions around state intervention, we must oppose it and build our own interventions via international solidarity. Only after serious changes and shifts in power can we hope to use the state as a force for positive intervention.

---

[70] Barbara Lee stands out as the only U.S. politician who voted against the War in Afghanistan from the beginning. See Lee 2008 for more context on her anti-war politics and connection to her earlier Black Panther work.

64

Principle 3: Pluralism (Anti-Hegemony)

Our third basic principle – pluralism – is about building a world where nations share power and no nation dominates others. Not even the U.S. will be able to maintain hegemonic or imperial domination in a pluralistic world. Pluralism is *not* about replacing U.S. hegemony with a different kind of hegemony. Nations that have dominated the world in the past – the British Empire, Spanish Empire – fared no better. Even nations dominant on a regional scale today do little better. The underlying issue, then, is one of power and the nation-state. It's not about individual nations, nor is the U.S. exceptionally bad compared to other imperial powers. The left can and should recognize that the current world will be much better – and leftist groups will have better conditions for organizing – when power between nations is much more balanced. This holds true regardless of which nations hold power at a given time. And so, it makes little sense to lionize opponents of the U.S. merely because they represent an alternative to the existing world framework. A Chinese empire, for example, represents no improvement over a U.S. one.

The left should work for a more pluralistic, multi-polar world. This is one where nations and regions share power in a background framework treating them as equally as possible. In the short-term, this means (selectively) supporting international institutions insofar as they limit U.S. hegemony. The International Criminal Court sometimes attempts to limit the abuses of the U.S. and its allies. For example, it launched an inquiry into war crimes committed during the 2003 U.S. invasion of Iraq[71]. The UN Charter contains provisions that – properly enforced – do so, too. Other international institutions and agreements limit the power of the U.S. and China – among other nations – to impose constraints on less powerful nations. For the most part, these international mechanisms are weak. We should encourage and strengthen these forces insofar as they serve the goals of advancing pluralism.

---

[71] See the ICC summary at: https://web.archive.org/web/20090327061739/http://www2.icc-cpi.int/NR/rdonlyres/F596D08D-D810-43A2-99BB-B899B9C5BCD2/277422/OTP_letter_to_senders_re_Iraq_9_February_2006.pdf. Last accessed: May 26, 2020.

Over the course of decades, the U.S. has taken action against many nations challenging U.S. hegemony or global capital. It has sponsored military coups in Chile, Guatemala, and Iran, among many other examples[72]. It supported a successful coup in Honduras and multiple unsuccessful ones in Venezuela. I'll cover many of these examples in Part II, particularly the U.S.'s history of intervention in Venezuela. But we can start from the point that strong international institutions provide a measure of cover and safety for leftist democratic experimentation. They particularly do so in less powerful nations. They keep the U.S. off their back long enough for them to work through key issues and problems.

In his book *A Foreign Policy for the Left*[73], longtime editor of *Dissent* magazine Michael Walzer argues for a pluralistic world largely on grounds of symmetry. He thinks the left should analyze politics from a perspective giving balance and equal weight to the wrongs of various countries. As a consequence, he argues the left should spend as much time and effort on the wrongs of Kim Jong-un's North Korean policy and Vladimir Putin's Russian policy as it does on Barack Obama's or Donald Trump's U.S. policy. For an example to which Walzer frequently appeals, he thinks leftists should spend as much time and effort critiquing Palestinian wrongs as Israeli ones. Walzer thinks some U.S. leftists over-react to American wrongs by praising anyone they see as enemies of the U.S. He cites – among other examples – leftist praise for U.S. rivals like Bashar al-Assad or Vladimir Putin. He thinks leftists praise them merely because they're opposed to the U.S. or to U.S. interests in specific cases[74]. Instead, Walzer favors an approach where the left criticizes U.S. imperialism but criticizes with equal force wrongdoing elsewhere.

While this all sounds plausible on its face, the principle of symmetry leads Walzer in very curious directions. He not only endorses U.S. wars

---

[72] This history is, again, extensive and widely discussed in the literature. Readers unfamiliar with the broad strokes would be advised to begin from Wikipedia's discussion: https://en.wikipedia.org/wiki/United_States_involvement_in_regime_change. Last accessed: May 26, 2020.

[73] Walzer 2018.

[74] Ibid., pp. 20-23.

in 1940s and 1950s Korea and 2000s Afghanistan[75], but he also endorses many of the goals of standard, textbook U.S. 'nation-building' projects[76]. Leaning too hard into symmetry leads the left into territory barely distinguishable from the liberal end of the bipartisan foreign policy consensus. It's an excellent case of seemingly enlightened principles having poor results. Our earlier discussion of anti-interventionism should also give readers some ideas about where these results come from. The poor results should lead us to re-examine what brought us there.

I think Walzer is correct that we shouldn't single out the U.S. for special *moral* critique. But his assumption of symmetry is *far* too strong. I'll have more to say about many of these specific cases in the Part II chapters on individual nations. But for now, there are two key reasons not to adopt symmetry as a principle. First, U.S. residents have far more influence on their own government – and the governments of close U.S. allies – than they do on governments of places like China, Russia, or Syria. Excessive time spent on the wrongs of 'enemy' or 'neutral' governments is ineffective at best. When it also enables U.S. wrongs, it's outright counterproductive. Certainly praising authoritarians like al-Assad or Putin is unwarranted, but one need not criticize them as much as, say, Obama or Trump. Second, while the U.S. isn't morally worse than these other states, it holds more power and therefore carries more potential to do harm. Thus, we need a critique of *power* and its uses rather than a critique of *morality*. Even if the U.S. is the moral equal – or even slight moral better – of some other country, it has far more power to enact its harmful policies. In most situations, we're justified in spending more time and effort criticizing U.S. interventionism than that of other nations.

What we need here is a world where there's a closer balance of power between nations, where no nation is able to exert its will over the planet. It's a problem when the U.S. does this, and it's a problem when any other nation does it. The difference for now is that the U.S. does it more easily and is therefore the largest problem. We're not going to create a revolution through the UN, either quickly or gradually. Nor will we create

---

[75] Ibid., pp. 28-29.
[76] Ibid., pp. 118-119.

one longer term merely through the use of foreign aid to leftist governments. But we can make selective use of these institutions in the shorter term to better balance world power. We can help create openings or spaces for the development of many different kinds of leftist movements and institutions – spaces for open, democratic experimentation. A more pluralistic world would better enable us to put in place the ideas we develop and learn through international solidarity.

Principle 4: Fighting Global Capital

Our fourth basic principle – fighting global capital – involves cooperation with our fellow workers across divisions of gender, nationality, race, et al. We do so to fight capital along its entire global supply chain. Capital is already a global movement. Companies have operated internationally for decades, and the economy was built for them to do so. This was the case even to some degree in the earliest stages of industrial capitalism. But especially in our era of financialized capitalism and tight competition over scarce resources, capital sharply increased its global operations. Supply chains moved from relatively domestic and lax to international and customized and hyper-accelerated. It's in fighting global capital where a left foreign policy bears obvious fruit and looks most analogous to our domestic policy consensus. Our fights against global capital build on the important work from the other three principles, and they do so through complex organization. It will involve: labor unions, broader organizations of workers, community groups and allies, tenants' groups, racial and gender justice groups, new international organizations, existing international systems, et al.

Despite the similarities to domestic policy, fighting global capital depends far more on our international connections. And it depends on these connections in multiple ways. One, the left must build connections among workers who are part of the same global supply chain. The products workers make and services they provide depend on materials and workers from around the globe. Even when they don't carry this dependence, companies could outsource them to another area. Thus, workers are rarely a self-contained unit. We've known this for decades in the manufacturing industry[77], but it's increasingly true in industries entirely domestic only a few decades ago. Building international links between labor groups is thus critical not only for long-term success – as it has always been – but often even for short-term success. Global supply chains are already a key component of existing labor battles in the U.S.

Two, this fight depends on the status of immigrants in the U.S. – our fights against the criminalization of borders and for high labor standards and immigrant access to social services regardless of legal status. Global capital wields the criminalization of borders and immigrants as a club against all workers. It uses the threat of deportation to prevent immigrants from organizing, holding them to low wages and poor working conditions. This, in turn, prevents non-immigrant workers from organizing and demanding good wages. A strong domestic labor alliance across immigrant status – built around opening borders and providing rights and services to *all*, regardless of immigration or legal status – benefits and strengthens all of us. I'll take up these issues in much more detail in Chapter 3.

In his book *Hired: Six Months Undercover in Low Wage Britain*[78], James Bloodworth studies precarious, low wage work and workers. He focuses most closely on industries enabled in the last few decades by global supply chains. He conducts his study in the UK, though it has international applications, and many of his cases involve U.S. companies or directly apply to low wage work in the U.S. Bloodworth builds his cases in a hands-on manner. He worked briefly in an Amazon Fulfillment Center, finding a largely Romanian immigrant workforce held to low wages and poor job conditions. Companies get away with this only because they hold serious legal and political leverage over immigrant workforces[79]. UK-born workers widely reject the terms of employment, but global capital – in the form of Amazon – uses the legal and political status of immigrants as a cudgel against *all* workers, both domestic and foreign.

---

[77] Readers looking for an extensive case study from the manufacturing industry would be well advised to consult Cowie 2001.

[78] Bloodworth 2018.

[79] Ibid., pp. 22-24.

Further cases range from discount store employment to ridesharing services. Here, Bloodworth finds that the legal status of immigrants and threats of law enforcement and punishment prevent immigrant workers from joining labor unions. These issues stretch across country of origin. He finds Polish immigrant workers in discount store employment[80] and South Asian workers in the London ridesharing industry[81]. In all three cases, he unearths coercive corporate behavior and class war against immigrants. Immigration law serves as the main tool while law enforcement serves as the main base of soldiers. And each case produces nativist, right-wing backlash against the immigrant workforce by native-born British workers. The backlash manifests itself in anti-immigrant attitudes and support for right-wing populist politicians. All this does its part to produce foolish policy moves like Brexit and constant weakening of minimum wage laws and other labor protections.

Bloodworth's cases shed light on the challenges and opportunities involved in fighting global capital. Major economic shifts over the previous two generations both displaced once-thriving industrial workforces and produced a new, immiserated immigrant labor force. And while doing these two things, the same forces extended supply chains around the globe in ways that further loosen connections between the site of work and the site of power. 'Just-in-time' production systems were the theory, and global supply chains the practice. But after forging new bonds of international solidarity and organizing workers across these divisions of space and identity, we will position ourselves to issue strong challenges to these vulnerable systems of capital. Stretched supply chains hold increasing weight, and 'just-in-time' production can be quickly made late. But the left must first put itself in position to take advantage of these new opportunities.

It will do so by organizing.

---

[80] Ibid., pp. 130-131.
[81] Ibid., pp. 229-256.

Putting Them Together

It should be clear that these four basic principles interrelate. International solidarity is often the prerequisite for any further useful action. By learning from one another and supporting one another, we start piecing together the information and practical know-how we need to build better movements. Anti-interventionism and pluralism are about creating space to build useful movements and allow these movements to grow without massive, hostile resistance. And fighting global capital is about putting it all together – using what we've learned and the spaces we've created to build a better world.

In Part II, we'll see how this plays out at the level of U.S. relations with other countries. How has the U.S. impacted the world, and how might a less interventionist, more pluralistic world benefit the left? Furthermore, how might we build movements and solidarity to bring this about? But before moving on to the discussion of U.S. relations with particular countries, let's look at an issue that fails to come to mind for many people when they think about foreign policy issues – immigration. We have an immigration system aimed at punishing workers from other nations to the alleged benefit of U.S. workers. But that's not how it works in practice. Let's look at the open borders debate. With these four principles in mind, I think it's much clearer how and why an open borders policy *helps* workers – both foreign and domestic. We can use these principles to join our fellow workers in other countries and work toward a more democratic system in all nations.

Chapter 3

Open Borders and the Left

When we put together these four basic principles – international solidarity, anti-interventionism, pluralism, and fighting global capital – we can do more as leftists. The principles clarify difficult issues for us, help us see the road ahead, and help us organize and build sustained movements. But they do something else for us that's far less obvious – they help us avoid foolish missteps and temptations. Certain political moves or stances might appeal to us at the outset even though they'd harm us in the long-term. We can use our basic principles to avoid these missteps.

I'll focus in this chapter on immigration issues, where we can see this idea in action. Many leftists oppose 'open borders' policies, and some leftists go a step further and outright oppose immigration. Most do so from a concern for the narrower, short-term interests of certain groups of U.S.-born workers. I'll argue that these anti-immigration stances are short-sighted, and I'll do so using our basic principles as a guide. I'll argue instead that a careful study of our basic principles recommends for us a leftist policy goal of open borders. And so, I'll argue in this chapter in favor of open borders. I'll show how we can use our four basic principles to build an integrated, internationalist left and distinguish the leftist case for open borders from the libertarian case for something they *call* 'open borders.'

Leftists and Libertarians

We know leftist opinion on open borders shifted in the last decade or so. Much of the left favors open borders whereas it once opposed them. Why? We see a convergence from many directions. At its 2019 National Convention, the DSA endorsed open borders in explicitly internationalist terms[82]. The resolution identified borders as a capitalist tool for separating working-class people into national rivalries. It pointed out the benefits of putting working people together, benefits including political education and solidarity. That's much of the *ideological* and *practical* ground for the shift, but political leadership also played a role. U.S. politicians like Julián Castro and Alexandria Ocasio-Cortez helped push the overall political landscape to the left on issues related to borders and immigration. They advocated policies to the left of the political mainstream, thereby expanding what's acceptable within the U.S. political system. And, in some cases, Americans simply adopted these policies because they came to *like* certain politicians, especially AOC and Bernie Sanders. Furthermore, pro-immigrant grassroots groups played an enormous role on the ground. More established groups like the League of United Latin American Citizens (LULAC) focus on legal and political advocacy for immigrants. They amplify efforts by funding specialized organizations such as the Mexican American Legal Defense and Education Fund. Newer groups – like Unidos US (formerly the National Council of La Raza) – push hard from the left on policy. And even yet more specialized groups like the National Immigration Forum and the Labor Council for Latin American Advancement push for policy and Latinx interests within organized labor, respectively.

This work creates a unity between Latinx interests, immigrant interests, and the moral intuitions of many Americans. Recent events also drive that unity. Support for immigrants on the left remained soft during the Obama years, but it slowly hardened. During the early Trump years,

---

[82]   https://proteanmag.com/2019/08/02/breaking-dsa-votes-to-endorse-open-borders-and-a-green-new-deal-program-at-atlanta-convention/ for coverage of the convention. Last accessed June 29, 2020. See early discussion of the resolution at: https://medium.com/@stevens.elijah/open-borders-resolution-dsa-national-convention-2019-28208937504. Last accessed June 29, 2020.

the U.S. press finally covered the oppression immigrants face as they try to cross the border and live their lives. And Trump fanned the flames with his words and policies. His travel bans, attempts to end DACA, and child separations policies all accelerated the rate at which the left moved toward pro-immigrant ideas. Some Trump immigration policies merely continued Obama era policy while others broke from that era. But they struck the broader public in new ways, partly due to the education and outreach efforts of Latinx and pro-immigrant groups. The net result? Americans know a lot more about mass deportation and inhumane treatment of immigrants than they did a decade ago. They pay greater attention to some of the routine U.S. border and internal ICE immigration policies the U.S. has carried out for years. We've moved the bar on what kinds of work the left does and might succeed at doing.

As with other elements of left foreign policy, much of this remains tentative. Ongoing political education and struggle remain key to making continued progress. We've seen anti-ICE protests and actions in many U.S. cities, certainly far more than we saw 10-15 years ago. We've even seen it here in Iowa, a state many Americans don't associate with immigration. A local group called the Center for Worker Justice of Eastern Iowa has built coalitions with local faith groups, civic groups, and non-profits to challenge local ICE activity[83]. But questions remain. Is this work sustainable at its current level, and how can we build it into something more powerful? Will the left continue building coalitions with a Democratic president in office who implements many of the same bad policies as Republicans? Will liberals and progressives ignore Democrats' anti-immigrant policies in the same ways they ignored Obama's? It all remains to be seen[84].

We can find among left-of-center immigration opponents both 'hard' and 'soft' anti-immigration stances. On the 'hard' side we find many

---

[83] See: https://cwjiowa.org/category/immigration/ for information on CWJ's pro-immigrant work. Last accessed June 29, 2020.

[84] That is to say, the liberal and leftist reaction to Joe Biden still largely remains to be seen. Biden's policy itself, on the other hand, has left us plenty to infer. See Lee 2021 for a discussion of very early Biden Administration immigration policy. Lee argues that, for the most part, Biden has acted (and will act) as a continuation of the Obama years.

mainstream labor groups prior to 2000. And on the 'soft' side, we find a messier picture. Many moderate and liberal Democrats take up the banner, and mainstream labor to this day largely still does. But we even find politicians further to the left who take soft anti-immigration stances, notably Bernie Sanders before about 2015 or 2016. We'll look at the hard and soft groups in turn, groups that come from very different perspectives and histories. Even accounting for these differences, though, we can find common concerns. They traveled these roads for some of the same reasons.

Mainstream labor led the charge on hard anti-immigration sentiment for most of the 20th century. Why? Many of its leaders saw immigrants as a threat to the jobs and wages of U.S.-born workers. Since U.S.-born workers – or at least a subset of them – constituted the membership and constituency of mainstream labor, they saw immigrants as a threat. As the reasoning goes, immigrants would flood the labor market with workers earning low wages. They'd crowd out native-born workers. Immigrants would disrupt the economic relations governing the employment market, namely the forces of supply and demand. Once *that* happens, U.S. workers must choose between taking pay and benefit cuts or joining the unemployment line. Organized labor thereby wanted to defend the economic interests of (part of) the U.S. working class. And it – or at least many of its mainstream components – chose to do so by backing restrictions on immigration.

Economic theory thus served as some of the underlying rationale. And – in fact – anti-immigrant sentiment had at least *some* connection to leftist analysis of capitalism. On this line of reasoning, capitalists want to create an 'industrial reserve army' of idle workers ready to replace workers who make trouble or price themselves out of the labor market with effective collective bargaining[85]. Immigrants would be a major part of this industrial reserve army. And so, labor didn't simply make it up wholescale out of prejudice, though, as we'll see, certain sorts of biases and prejudices played a role. However, the economics weren't as simple as some labor leaders suggested. Many Marxists themselves disagreed strongly with the

---

[85] This idea dates to Karl Marx. See Marx 1990 [1867], pp. 781-794.

'Marxist' point about the industrial reserve army. David Harvey, for example, points out that capitalism *doesn't* want a labor force that's *completely* mobile. With a total ability for free movement, it would be difficult for capitalists to keep immigrant workers in place. They'd demand something better than low-wage work, and if they didn't get it, they'd move on to somewhere else[86]. I'll return to this point later when discussing Suzy Lee's argument for open borders.

And so, we must take care not to exaggerate the direct role of economic theory. Anti-immigrant labor groups didn't represent the *entire* working class. They mostly represented 'high-skill' industrial laborers. Indeed, they excluded many more marginalized workers: agricultural workers, service workers, temp and part-time workers, various 'low-skilled' workers, unemployed workers, and so on[87]. Racism played a role in these exclusions, as did the law. Others they excluded because it was difficult to organize the workers and/or they didn't want to try[88]. Of course, we can discuss the various impacts of discrimination and racism. But one obvious implication is that mainstream labor only represented part of the working class. For this reason, achieving the material interests of their members wouldn't necessarily achieve the material interests of the working class *as a whole*. In cases of conflicts of interests – or incompleteness of interests – labor sometimes fell short. Immigration policy is one major example of many labor groups falling short.

Conflicts and tensions throughout U.S. labor history form the biggest factor leading to mainstream labor's increasing sympathy to immigrants. This history forms a positive feedback loop. Conflicts and social forces expanded the range of workers labor unions cover. As a result, more people shared in the benefits and successes of labor actions. Labor then further expanded the range of workers in its reach. Most importantly for

---

[86] See Harvey 2018 [1982], pp. 165-166.

[87] On this topic, see Coates 2017. Ta-Nehisi Coates points out that – among other means of exclusion – U.S. law explicitly excluded certain workers in its labor law. See also Touré Reed's reply to Coates: https://catalyst-journal.com/vol1/no4/between-obama-and-coates. Reed complicates the picture quite a bit.

[88] https://www.npr.org/2013/02/05/171175054/how-the-labor-movement-did-a-180-on-immigration. Last accessed: October 22, 2020.

this point, different types of people – not just white, male, industrial workers – joined in these successes, changing the composition of labor groups over time. More Latinx workers and service workers, for example, joined unions. Due to these changes, large groups of unions – particularly the AFL-CIO – changed their approach to immigration by 2000. More AFL-CIO members were immigrants or people from immigrant families. Labor groups remained, as always, responsive to some degree to their own membership.

These broader forces had as much impact as economic theory, if not more. Indeed, the very *survival* of the labor movement in the early 21st century probably depended on becoming more responsive to immigrants and Latinx workers. The U.S. working class is more black, more Latinx, and more service sector based than it was 50-70 years ago. It was never acceptable to represent only white, male, industrial workers. But in 2021, doing such a thing might not even be *survivable* for a union. To stay relevant, unions had to change. They had to become more inclusive – both in terms of demographics and economic sectors – and they had to adapt on immigration policy in order to engage more workers. Beyond this, including a wider range of workers – and remaining democratically responsive to that membership – produced even further changes.

In fact, some of the economic issues remained the same. Labor leaders still came largely from the industrial sectors, and some still believed immigrants harmed native-born workers. But labor leaders cut a pragmatic deal. By focusing on immigrant rights, they believed they could raise working conditions for *everyone*. A focus on immigrant rights might thereby prevent the de-valuing of work and lowering of wages. This, too, was controversial on the left. Marxists were never especially convinced by the 'supply and demand' reasoning underlying this entire perspective. From a Marxist perspective, wages depend on the value of workers' labor power. And *that* value involves a complicated social relationship. Among other things, it depends on: the standard of living society deems acceptable, the costs of raising children, job skills and training, unemployment levels, and even the state of a nation's social development. It's not simply a matter of supply and demand, which Marxists interpret as largely without explanatory value. Immigrants thus receive low wages not because they flood the market, but rather because society places a lower premium on their lives and work. It's important to counter these forces by building closer links with immigrants, helping U.S.-born workers see them as full Americans with the same value as anyone else[89].

Let's move on to consider softer anti-immigration views and the right-wing views they engage with. Softer anti-immigration leftists still accept the assumption that a large immigrant workforce harms U.S.-born workers. They also tend to focus on immigrant rights, trying – as outlined above – to lift standards for all. To see this in action, let's return to Bernie Sanders. By 2020, Sanders became a leader on pro-immigrant policy. But as recently as 5-10 years prior, he was anything but a leader. He held a 'soft' anti-immigration view, and he said so explicitly. Sanders voted against multiple reform bills and opposed a diversity lottery. Many on the left joined Sanders for largely the same reasons, including some Latinx groups like LULAC[90]. Thus, soft anti-immigration figures ground their views in misguided pro-U.S. worker sentiment. They often combine it with genuine concern for immigrants coming to the U.S. for asylum or other humanitarian reasons. Despite holding a soft anti-immigration stance, Sanders has consistently opposed immigrant detention throughout his career, and he regularly voted against punitive legislation.

Why do soft anti-immigration politicians balk at going full pro-immigrant? Some of them hold reservations about 'open borders' – both the term and the policy. They speak inclusively about immigrant rights, but they draw a line at open borders. One reason behind this reservation is the view that right-wingers – particularly libertarians – push open borders as part of their agenda. Indeed, libertarians often talk this way. They've said for many years they favor what they *call* 'open borders.' If the U.S. left favors open borders as well, it *must* distinguish its position from

---

[89] There's much more to say about Marx's views on the value of labor power and wages, and there's plenty of disagreement within Marxist circles. For an accessible discussion of these issues, I'd highly recommend Harvey 2018 [1982], especially pp. 45-49 and 55-57. Harvey's discussion forms much of the basis for my own reading of Marx on these issues.

[90] See: https://www.vox.com/policy-and-politics/2020/2/25/21143931/bernie-sanders-immigration-record-explained. Last accessed: July 29, 2020.

that of libertarians. Improving leftist policy and explaining the difference between leftism and libertarianism stand out as two key goals.

Libertarians aim their 'open borders' rhetoric at the free movement of capital and labor across political boundaries. They say they want both capital and labor to move where they want and conduct business wherever and in whatever way they'd like. This is, in fact, a preventative argument. Libertarians want to prevent the state from stopping businesses and people from crossing borders. There's no suggestion anywhere that libertarians support *positive* measures for immigrants. They don't support additional social services, education, housing, and so on. Unlike the AFL-CIO, Sanders, and other left-leaning soft anti-immigration forces, libertarians are ultimately concerned about *capital*, not labor. They include both in their rhetoric, but they only support one side in practice. It's far easier for capital to cross borders than for labor to do so. Libertarians thus want a world where businesses hire who they want, when they want, and at what price they want. Holding people back from social services forces them into dependence on low-wage work. It's these latter reasons why people like Charles Koch work with moderate Republicans and moderate and liberal Democrats on immigration legislation. And it's why the AFL-CIO and Sanders remain skeptical of that legislation[91].

As we'll see, fighting immigrants isn't the way to oppose libertarians. Neither 'hard' nor 'soft' anti-immigration sentiment ultimately benefits the left. It's better to work together with immigrants. And 'open borders' is the slogan that organizes this work. Open borders are the avenue for coalitions and solidarity.

What Are Open Borders?

We can find examples of both Democrats and Republicans who want to liberalize immigration law[92]. Almost all Democrats advocate an easier path to citizenship for immigrants already in the U.S. Among other things, this includes an extension of DACA and a rollback of much of Trump's far

---

[91] See: https://time.com/5491587/koch-brothers-network-immigration-reform/. Last accessed June 29, 2020.

[92] See Feldman 2020 on the inadequacies of both Democratic and Republican proposals.

right immigration policies. Even on the Republican side, George W. Bush endorsed a version of a path to citizenship. His ideas aren't much different from those most Democrats and more than a few Republicans endorse. And so, there are parts of mainstream U.S. politics standing outside Trump's extreme anti-immigrant rhetoric, even if there's crossover on certain elements of policy.

In principle, deciding whether to have open or closed borders is a different issue from all this. We can distinguish between open borders, on the one hand, and citizenship and basic humane treatment of immigrants, on the other. The citizenship and treatment questions appear to amount to matters of basic human decency in the enforcement of laws, whereas open borders appear to move beyond all this. But it doesn't work this way in practice. The U.S. has overlapping law enforcement agencies working on immigration issues, and it has little in the way of strong oversight of these agencies. U.S. law enforcement carries a deep history of racist abuse, and the entire law enforcement system rests on racist foundations[93]. Simply changing a few citizenship laws or curbing excessive enforcement probably won't accomplish a great deal except at the margins. For these reasons, 'open borders' sits politically to the left of enforcement reform and humane treatment on the U.S. political spectrum. The U.S. left case is that only through the kind of deep, systemic change created by open borders will we be able to modify the system sufficiently to improve the lives of immigrants – and everyone else.

As a result, we might think about open borders as a step beyond what liberal or progressive Democrats advocate. We can provisionally define 'open borders' as a policy removing major legal controls on movement across borders. At one extreme, we might totally eliminate checkpoints at borders. But at the other extreme, we might have a policy of heavy border checkpoints that merely lack criminal enforcement. On this definition, for much of U.S. history open borders were the norm. Indeed, until well into the 19th century, U.S. immigration policy looked like the 'no checkpoints' version. There were few regulations at all, and the U.S. opened its doors

---

[93] On the foundations question, I'd highly recommend leftists new to prison abolitionism check out the study guide from Abolition journal: https://abolitionjournal.org/studyguide/.

to anyone who wanted to come. With that said, the U.S. was hardly a paradise for immigrants. It didn't provide many social services or support to immigrants, and it obviously still had a system of slavery. However, it did allow most immigrants to enter and stay.

Let's look at a couple of examples of open borders policies from elsewhere. We'll start with the India-Nepal Treaty of Peace and Friendship of 1950[94]. The treaty established full rights of residence, property ownership, and economic and trade participation within both countries. It did so symmetrically, including citizens of either nation. In effect, this meant that citizens of India and citizens of Nepal could freely move between the two nations. Some elements of the Nepalese left – particularly Maoist groups – criticized the treaty, remaining skeptical of wealthy Indian business owners and visitors. There have also been various points at which one country or the other ignored treaty elements. But the treaty itself held for decades. It's only in the last decade or so that India and Nepal have seriously considered scrapping it. For a second example, let's look at the Schengen Agreement among European nations. It was an earlier, regional agreement later folded in to the European Union. The idea was to begin from a few nations in central and western Europe, gradually reduce border checks, and expand to other nations. The agreement also provided for easier travel between European nations. Agreements like this one – and the earlier Nordic Passport Union[95] among Scandinavian nations – are limited in comparison to the India-Nepal Treaty. In some cases, they really provide legal protection only for travel. The Nordic Passport Union required people to show a passport for employment or social services. These latter cases, then, are at the other extreme. If they count as 'open borders' policies at all, they're the minimal version.

---

[94] For a basic overview here, the relevant Wikipedia entry serves well enough: https://en.wikipedia.org/wiki/1950_Indo-Nepal_Treaty_of_Peace_and_Friendship.____ Last accessed July 29, 2020.

[95] These are two further examples where, again, the Wikipedia entries serve quite well to introduce the reader: https://en.wikipedia.org/wiki/Schengen_Agreement; https://en.wikipedia.org/wiki/Nordic_Passport_Union. Both last accessed: July 29, 2020.

In the U.S., people who advocate for open borders tend to have something in mind closer to the Schengen Agreement than the India-Nepal Treaty. Most want to abolish enforcement mechanisms, and then build on that abolition to change the actual border regulatory structure. We find advocacy for ending enforcement with examples like the 'Abolish ICE' slogan. Abolishing ICE would do precisely what it suggests, namely abolish an enforcement mechanism from U.S. law. If that's the only thing it would do, then it wouldn't change much about the legal structure itself. It would also leave intact other forms of legal enforcement. U.S. Customs and Border Protection, which handles enforcement at borders, serves as a good example of an enforcement agency that's not part of ICE and would need to be addressed separately. On their own, these ideas hardly meet any standard for 'open borders.' But open borders advocates might see these ideas as a stepping stone or as a key part of a larger reform package.

2020 presidential candidate Julián Castro introduced a sweeping immigration reform plan. The plan arguably qualified as 'open borders' at the softer end of the spectrum. This is surprising for a couple of reasons. First, Castro previously spent much of his career as a mainstream Democrat, barely even qualifying as a liberal by our definitions in Chapter 1. He leapt rather drastically to the left when running a national campaign. Second, Democrats had shown little previous inclination to move beyond criticizing Trump on immigration. And so, the political landscape shifted further to the left than expected. Castro's plan would have broken down much of ICE's enforcement power, but – perhaps more importantly – it would have overturned the 1929 law that criminalized illegal entry into the country[96]. This law forms the underlying legal basis for U.S. immigration policy. It's this component that pushed Castro's plan into 'open borders' territory. It wouldn't formally open the borders in the way we find in, e.g., the Nordic countries, but it would more or less end the criminalization of immigration.

All this means the U.S. left faces some choices. 'Open borders' is more slogan than policy. This is also quite true of 'Abolish ICE.' We can't enact

---

[96]   https://www.vox.com/2019/4/2/18291584/2020-immigration-democrats-policy-castro-abolish-ice. Last accessed: July 29, 2020.

open borders merely with a simple law or executive order. In fact, we have to think about what form it should take. The U.S. left must do so with careful deliberation, democratic inclusion, and openness.

Lee's Argument for Open Borders

In a 2019 article in *Catalyst*[97], Suzy Lee presented a leftist argument for open borders. She sketched it out as an organizing goal for the U.S. left. I think her argument provides a great starting point for discussion, both in this book and in leftist movements. I'll sketch out Lee's reasoning as I interpret it. Then, I'll offer a more extensive discussion around the topic. I'll focus in particular on how open borders – both as a goal and a reality – will help us create an international left. It aligns well to our four basic principles and shows them in action.

Here's how I read the basic structure of Lee's argument:

1. Immigration flow and immigrant rights are separate issues, and it's important to distinguish between them. But the two concepts closely relate, politically. In today's neoliberal capitalism, it's necessary – but not sufficient – to achieve immigration flow in order to achieve immigrant rights.

2. Leftist projects require achieving immigrant rights. Immigrants work in key industries. Thus, to build strong unions and worker power at key points in the capitalist system the left must organize immigrant workers.

3. As a consequence of (1), the left must achieve a legal path for immigration flow. It must do so in order to make the gains in immigrant rights needed for the projects in (2).

4. Fighting for open borders is the best way to achieve immigration flow in a way that opens the door for immigrant rights.

---

[97] Lee 2019.

5. Therefore, the left should endorse and work toward open borders.

Lee's distinction between immigration flow and immigrant rights serves as the lynchpin for her broader argument. We'll start by laying this out. The 'soft anti-immigration' folks I mentioned earlier conflate these two things. They don't draw a distinction between flow and rights. This is also a key problem with libertarian reasoning, and it's one reason why the left can't accept libertarian views. Even worse, people who make this conflation often adopt the misconception that *capital* is in favor of immigrant rights. And so, we have to start by carefully laying out and examining the distinction. It's key to how labor and leftist positions differ from these others.

Capital wants *flow* over and above *rights*. In fact, it prefers flow to the *exclusion* of rights. Why? Businesses need immigrant labor. Thus, they need immigrant laborers who move in and out of the country, which is what 'flow' amounts to. Furthermore, Lee points out that this need isn't constant over time. General technological advances – particularly automation – reduce capital's need for immigrant labor over time. While exceptions occur, the general need for immigrant labor trends down. U.S. business doesn't depend on immigrant labor to the degree it did in lower tech, more industrial periods 80-100 years ago[98]. Given its greater labor needs in earlier decades, capital allowed a higher level of immigrant rights, and it did so for purely pragmatic reasons. It wanted access to more labor, and it made concessions to gain that access. More recently – given lower levels of labor needs – capital no longer makes concessions on immigrant rights. According to Lee, this stands out as a key reason why the U.S. regulates immigration more heavily in the 21st century than in the late 19th or early 20th centuries.

---

[98] In a more recent issue of *Catalyst*, there's a detailed debate between David B. Feldman and Suzy Lee over a number of issues. But one issue on which they disagree is the idea that capital's demand for immigrant labor has declined over time. Feldman points to rebounds in the percentage of immigrant population in the U.S. since 1970. Lee claims this doesn't get at the full story, and she cites instead the distribution of workers across industries. Lee's basic claim is that immigrant labor – where it exists in the 21st century – is more heavily concentrated in industries where capital does not have an interest in compromising on its opposition to immigrant rights.

And so, capital's need for immigration flow doesn't always extend to immigrant rights. Indeed, it's now quite the opposite. Businesses use immigration restrictions to intensify labor and hold down wages. Furthermore, all this serves as a key lever for capital. Immigrants in the 21st century heavily work in the service sector and other industries with certain key features. They're the industries where it's most difficult to use automated tools, intensify labor, and use others means to extract as much value from workers as possible in a short time period. By making workers afraid of deportation and evading labor law, capital extracts the most value it can in a challenging situation. This is all very compatible with Harvey's reading of Marx I cited earlier. Capitalists need access to workers, but this need declines over time with more productivity. Excess worker mobility is contrary to capitalist interests, explaining why capital doesn't want workers to freely flow in and out of the U.S. without constraint. Therefore, capital creates a system to capture and threaten workers, maintaining access to the labor they still need and maximizing the extraction of value.

With the distinction in hand, we can understand the first part of Lee's argument. Immigration flow is necessary, but not sufficient, for achieving immigrant rights. By closely looking at the history of labor, we see that flow and rights can be pried apart. How? Capital created a system allowing it to bring in workers without giving them rights. Not only this, but it's probably not possible to give workers rights without securing flow. In practice, the very right to exist in a space is needed to make immigrant rights meaningful and enforceable. We have to treat people as full persons before thinking seriously about their rights. This latter point severely undermines the attitudes of some of the labor leaders and politicians we discussed earlier.

In her later premises, Lee establishes the close connection between immigration flow and leftist goals. Not that this should be controversial to the left. Much of the U.S. left already sees the need for immigrant rights. Lee claims the left emphasizes rights over flow, and she claims this is a mistake. How did this happen? How did the left come to emphasize rights over flow? For one, immigrant rights *are* important, and the left recognized this. The left has long understood raising working standards for *anyone* will protect *everyone*. By contrast, the political and economic context made it more difficult to understand the importance of flow. It was controversial within leftist and union circles for the reasons we discussed above. Unions worried flow would cost members' jobs. For these reasons, simple pragmatism dictated a focus on rights over flow. Rights benefit everyone, while flow – on the misguided way unions understood it – benefit only a few.

However, it's simply not true that flow only benefits a few. Lee argues it's far more complex than this. For one, it's tough for immigrants to have rights when they aren't safe in the country[99]. Flow, via legal status, therefore stands out as a precondition for genuine immigrant rights. And so, many leftists missed an important connection. But Lee adds a second point. Our current era of neoliberal capitalism concentrates immigrant labor in areas difficult to automate or outsource. This includes, among other areas: agriculture, construction, and personal services. These jobs will stick around. For the U.S. left, unionizing these industries is therefore extremely valuable. It would provide the working class much needed leverage in its class struggle with capital. Immigrants also comprise a larger and larger portion of the U.S. working class as a whole. Whatever benefits immigrants therefore benefits the entire working class in multiple ways.

This stands out as a pressing issue because these industries currently have low unionization rates. Hence, the U.S. working class leaves great power on the table. Restrictions on immigration flow cause some of these low rates. Workers fear ICE raids, deportation, and so on, fear that prevents them from organizing with their fellow workers. Removing that threat produces better conditions for unionization. As these industries continue growing – and as immigrant workers join unions in greater

---

[99] Feldman 2020 attempts to respond to Lee's point on the grounds that advocacy for a robust 'amnesty' program might achieve these goals more effectively than advocacy for open borders. Lee 2020 responds by claiming that 'amnesty,' too, is nebulous and unclear. She doesn't think it offers any significant advantages and that it probably offers disadvantages in the sense that it's not as strong a program. On this issue, I find Lee to be largely correct. Any political terminology or slogan can be appropriated and distorted by the political right. Allowing this possibility to govern left strategy is mistaken unless one can provide very strong reasons for doing it.

numbers – immigrants become a key strategic part of the working-class alliances needed for leftist movements to thrive.

Finally, there's a third point Lee doesn't mention. Immigrants have always made up a large part of leftist movements. This is true in the U.S., but it's also true in many other places. And the benefits don't stop with immigrants. The *children* of immigrants also stand out as key to leftist movements. The benefits, then, accrue to the left across multiple generations. Latinx organizers do some of the best organizing in the U.S. That's even true here in Iowa, which most people think about as an overwhelmingly white state. Many historical U.S. socialist leaders were immigrants or the children of immigrants, including Eugene V. Debs himself[100]. Flow builds solidarity. And it builds solidarity in multiple senses – more lived experience, better connections, a better intellectual base, et al.

Open Borders and Leftist Movements

The U.S. left wants to build a movement centered on all working-class people and concerns. People of color long made up a large portion of the potential U.S. working-class coalition. But the portion grows still larger today, and the left increasingly recognizes this fact. The left cannot – and largely *does not* – share the media's fixation with the 'white working class.' We see this all across the resurgent U.S. left, perhaps most notably in the 2020 Sanders campaign. However, this is a multi-racial coalition, and the coalition does include white workers. When discussing open borders, the left's challenge is to turn the multi-racial nature of the working-class coalition into a *strength* – to use racial diversity to make everyone stronger. How can we do that?

Lee frames the task through the existing union structure. She cites evidence showing 'low skill' white workers are concerned about their economic prospects and that they also hold anti-immigrant sentiments[101]. She thinks unions act as a counterbalance, forming a key part of an anti-

---

[100] Eugene V. Debs, as many know, ran multiple campaigns for president on the Socialist Party of America ticket and twice one nearly a million votes. But, as fewer people know, Debs was born to French immigrants to the U.S.

[101] Lee 2019, pp. 31–34.

nativist strategy[102]. Union leaders and organizers, so the thinking goes, hold more progressive views. If they spread the union message and unite people in collective struggle, they'll bring in more white workers and improve the workers' attitudes. I think Lee gets at something important, but there's also a role here for other forces. I'd cite political education and struggle extending beyond one's own workplace. Workers aren't just workers. They're tenants, consumers, voters, and many other things. The left can build multi-racial coalitions around many of these things, many of the sites where working-class people come together across racial lines. As a tenants union organizer myself, I find tenants to be a promising group. In fact, tenants gain great knowledge from their experience renting the places they live. We know landlords put the squeeze on tenants of all races and genders, but we also know landlords enact racist and sexist behavior. Even in the workplace itself, unionization and worker sentiment must come together more organically. Political education run by a few union organizers probably won't succeed. What we need is a careful dialogue between workers and organizers both inside and outside the company[103].

The call for open borders provides the left with an excellent starting point for this project. It's straightforward and easy to understand. It gels with people's moral intuitions toward openness. And it shares these features with ideas from the left's domestic agenda, particularly around health care and housing. Finally, as we'll see, our four basic principles strongly recommend the call for open borders.

Done well, the demand for open borders critically involves building international solidarity. It's simply an essential feature of the work we do toward open borders. Immigrants come to the U.S. from many places, and they often move back and forth. Most immigrants have family members who remain in their birth country. When U.S.-born workers build links with immigrant workers – and when U.S. unions welcome immigrant members as full members – they thereby build bonds of solidarity with multi-national families. It's simply baked into the relationship. This

---

[102] Ibid., pp. 34-38.

[103] We particularly saw the need for this when numerous prominent union leaders stood up to oppose including the Bernie Sanders and Pramila Jayapal Medicare for All proposal in the 2020 Democratic platform.

provides the left with yet another reason to focus on immigrant workers. Any bond between immigrant and union is usually an international bond.

With these bonds built, immigrant and native-born workers learn from one another. Immigrants join the union and contribute to it. Among other things, they learn about issues concerning U.S. foreign policy. In turn, U.S.-born workers learn first-hand about the negative impact of U.S. interventionism. And it's often the first opportunity they've had to learn in this way. We saw in Chapter 2 – by reviewing Jessica Trisko Darden's work – that the U.S. relies on the ignorance of its own population to maintain support for interventionism. It does so especially around lower profile forms of intervention like foreign aid. All this creates a stable system, but the system remains susceptible to people who break through the fog of ignorance surrounding foreign policy. The relationships created through more open borders are exactly the kind of thing that can perform this task.

Finally, the call for open borders can help with initial steps toward pluralism and fighting global capital. Open borders create a more welcoming environment and make it easier and safer for immigrants to join unions. Implicit in all this is a greater equality and flatter hierarchy between U.S.-born and foreign-born Americans. Putting people in more egalitarian relationships moves us a bit closer toward pluralism[104]. Furthermore, putting people together in collective struggle on the same footing helps them more effectively fight global capital. And when these struggles build over time, such as with the Central American solidarity movement, the left makes greater gains. At the start, movements have to overcome barriers between people. But once they've done this, and put together a broad coalition, unwinnable fights become winnable. For these reasons, open borders facilitate a wide range of what the left does and wants to do. We need open borders to form better bonds of international solidarity that change our actions and put us on a more equal footing. And when we do these things, the fight against global capital becomes possible and victory becomes attainable.

---

[104] There's also the possibility of open borders promoting more effective systems of global governance. See Chen 2020 for a leftist defense of open borders along these lines.

Open Borders and COVID-19

COVID-19 changed a lot about life in the U.S., and it did so quickly. Indeed, it changed the entire world, but failed politics in the U.S. heightened the severity here. In some cases, COVID reverted Americans to old, ingrained attitudes and patterns. Crises alienate people from their fellow workers, and COVID sent some workers back to anti-immigrant attitudes. Organizers encountered practical problems as well. As a tenants union organizer, I found it incredibly difficult to deal with the lack of in-person conversation. Despite tech industry claims to the contrary, you can't do all the things with video chat you can do in-person. One-on-one conversations remain the bread-and-butter of organizing, and organizers need new strategies to deal with these challenges. Anti-immigrant sentiments – and anti-Chinese and anti-Asian attitudes in particular – stand out as an ongoing concern. The best way to fight these problems is to inoculate ourselves and our fellow workers before disaster strikes. Reactive moves after the fact can't quite reach the same level of effectiveness. And so, COVID-19 highlights the great need to build sustained political education programs. We have neither substitute nor shortcut.

I think we can sketch out a basic political education narrative for immigration in the era of COVID-19 and global pandemics. Some people assert that open borders spread disease, but the reality remains quite the opposite. U.S. policy calls for the detention and concentration of immigrants. Rather than prevent problems, this in fact *advances* the spread of disease. COVID-19 spread like wildfire through many detention facilities, from immigrant detention to broader prison detention. These detention facilities did not protect the broader community. Why? No detention facility is ever closed. They remain linked to communities whether people acknowledge it or not. Where there's disease spread in one, it'll cross over to the other. Beyond this, immigrant workers tend to be heavily concentrated in industries – like the meatpacking industry here in Iowa – where COVID-19 spread was heaviest. While there are many reasons behind this, a lack of immigrant rights is a big part. Closed border policies and enforcement spread disease.

While it's easy to impart this information *intellectually*, it's important to reinforce it with organizing and solidarity. The idea that open borders promote disease feels intuitive to some people. But that remains largely an illusion. It feels most intuitive to people who don't *know* immigrants. It's the view of people who don't see themselves as having interests in common with immigrants. A good leftist program, by contrast, brings people together. It overcomes these barriers between workers to advance a better message. The open borders debate thereby breaks down the barriers capital uses to separate workers from one another and from leftist ideas. It thus holds a place of major importance to the U.S. left. Unfortunately, we don't yet discuss it in a way that matches its importance. That must change.

While my main focus in this book is issues of war and peace, I've considered in this chapter an issue many of us don't think about as part of foreign policy. But we should. It's too important an issue for us to marginalize. My focus on war and peace will be evident as we move on to Part II. But we should always keep issues of immigration in mind.

Part II

Around the World

We have got on to slippery ice where there is no friction, and so, in a certain sense, the conditions are ideal; but also, just because of that, we are unable to walk. We want to walk: so we need *friction*. Back to the rough ground!

Ludwig Wittgenstein, *Philosophical Investigations*

Chapter 4

Latin America

In Part II, we'll consider four key regions for U.S. foreign policy, beginning in this chapter with Latin America. I'll provide an overview of U.S. Latin America policy through the examples of U.S. policy toward Venezuela and Bolivia. There are a couple of key reasons why Venezuela and Bolivia provide deeper insight into the region. First, the Pink Tide movement – combining grassroots and Indigenous organizing with social democratic politics – looms large over recent Latin American politics[105]. Venezuela was an early, influential example of the Pink Tide, and Bolivia best integrated Indigenous organizing into politics in the Pink Tide era. Second, these two nations represent the most promising challenges to global capital in the region. Venezuela's '21st century socialism' provided a promising vision for a non-capitalist alternative, and its Bolivarian government organized a number of key regional institutions. Bolivia, in turn, refined some of the problems with the Venezuelan model. It represents the starkest contrast between a democratic and impoverished Indigenous-led population, on the one hand, and a small, wealthy elite, on the other. Together, these cases will provide a sense of direction for the U.S. left in its organizing efforts.

As we discussed in Chapter 2, the U.S. has a deep and troubling history of interference in Latin American affairs. This dates to the Monroe

---

[105] Readers looking for a close discussion of the Pink Tide movement from a leftist perspective should consult Gonzalez 2018. Readers looking for a more cultural perspective and a look at broader alliances in Latin America should consult Gomez-Barris 2018.

Doctrine, but it evolved over time. The U.S. once claimed anti-colonial attitudes, strongly opposing European colonialism in the Americas in its 19th century Latin America policy. Of course, it did so due to rivalry with European empires rather than any desire for autonomy or justice for Latin American people. The U.S. did not want half a dozen European empires roaming within easy reach of the U.S. mainland, and so anti-colonialism became a useful policy frame. The U.S. then began its own empire-building in the late 19th and early 20th centuries. To support these efforts, it expanded the Monroe Doctrine into something excusing its at-will interference in the affairs of other nations in the Western Hemisphere. To this day, U.S. policy retains much of this reworking of the Monroe Doctrine. Mainstream U.S. foreign policy still allows for free interference in the affairs of Latin American nations.

Venezuela and The Left

Venezuela presented one of the strongest challenges to global capital in the early 21st century. Internally, it also saw a dizzying array of coup attempts and other shenanigans. Unsurprisingly, the two phenomena relate to one another. We find few U.S. fingerprints directly on the shenanigans, but the U.S. remains close to all of these events. The coups range from carefully plotted to frightfully slapstick, from a nearly successful 2002 general strike to the shameless failures of the 2019 Juan Guaidó coup and 2020 ham-fisted invasion[106] by a couple of former U.S. soldiers. Despite the differences, we find common themes. Each Venezuelan coup was in its own way designed to do capital's dirty work. Capital remains quite upset by current events in the nation, and Venezuela inspires similar events throughout the region and the world. Due to these factors, Venezuela remains a hot spot for potential U.S. intervention.

I'll start this section with an overview of Venezuela's 20th century history, an overview highlighting the backdrops for recent crises and the U.S.'s continuing role. Next, I'll examine more recent events and draw

---

[106]   See: https://www.aljazeera.com/news/2020/05/venezuela-failed-coup-plot-200506073924677.html. Last accessed May 15, 2020.

inferences about Venezuela's future prospects. Closely studying these prospects will allow the U.S. left to better build international solidarity with the Venezuelan left. Finally, I'll conclude with an assessment of U.S. policy through the lens of our four basic principles. All four principles apply to U.S. policy in Venezuela. In fact, they complement one another nicely. But international solidarity and non-interventionism come together to provide the most important lessons. It's through focusing on these two principles that the U.S. left will put forward the best future vision.

In looking at the current situation, what a wide range of attitudes toward Venezuela we find on the U.S. left! Furthermore, these attitudes hint at deeper divisions within the U.S. left itself. We might think of it as a spectrum. At one end, some believe Hugo Chávez did nothing wrong, except perhaps practice too much modesty. And at the other end, others believe there's little Chávez did right, except perhaps put in place a few social democratic reforms. For the former group, Chávez blazed a revolutionary path toward socialism. And for the latter group, capitalism doesn't sound so bad in the short-term. Who are the combatants here? On the former side, we find people like former London mayor Ken Livingstone and U.S. academic George Ciccariello-Maher[107]. They take a combative and provocative approach to politics, to put it mildly. Both embrace some kind of maximalism, and both – especially Ciccariello-Maher – do so as a part of a social media brand. Livingstone gets right to the point. In an interview[108], he cited Chávez's failure to "kill all the oligarchs" as the reason for recent problems in the country. On the latter side, we find people like Nathan J. Robinson (*Current Affairs*) and Bhaskar Sunkara (*Jacobin*). They want to introduce gradual, electoral socialist movements to broad U.S. audiences, explicitly associating themselves with the 2016 and 2020 Bernie Sanders campaigns. For them, Venezuela

---

[107] For an overview of Ciccariello-Maher's approach to Venezuelan leftist politics, see Ciccariello-Maher 2013.

[108] See: https://www.theguardian.com/politics/2017/aug/03/ken-livingstone-venezuela-crisis-hugo-chavez-oligarchs. Last accessed May 15, 2020.

is something of an obstacle to people joining the movement. It scares people away, and they usually avoid discussing it[109].

U.S. leftists bring a wide range of projects and concerns to the table here. That's fine. For *this* project, we *need* to address Venezuela. And we need to do so clearly, comprehensively, and directly. The country offers for us both lessons and notes of caution. And many new leftists carry little beyond what they've read in a popular article or newspaper. We find, then, no broad consensus on Venezuela. Insofar as we do find one, it's perhaps this: vague criticism of Donald Trump and possibly Barack Obama or Joe Biden, vague opposition to coups, and special critique reserved for any potential U.S. involvement in war. This provides us with little in the way of a starting point. War remains only a vague future prospect, except for its brief appearances in the news. But, in fact, we're already close to war. We should start by reviewing how we got there and how U.S. policy promotes the interests of both Venezuelan and U.S. capital.

Representative Democracy and Disruption

Like much of Latin America, Venezuela spent the bulk of the 20th century as a representative democracy. At least on paper. It organized its democracy around the Puntofijo Pact, an agreement to set aside armed conflict and one-party rule in order to preserve the country's economic and political system. This system comprised three major political parties – Democratic Action (Acción Democrática), COPEI (Partido Socialcristiano), and Democratic Republican Union (Unión Republicana Democrática) – Venezuelan capital, and even the occasional left-wing populist leader[110]. And it made for a very stable system. But 'stable' doesn't translate to 'good' or even 'adequate.' When the U.S. promotes what it calls 'stability,' 'stability' means preservation of U.S. interests in

---

[109] See Robinson 2019 and Sunkara 2019. While both address foreign policy issues to some extent, neither discusses Venezuela in any depth. Indeed, there's no entry for 'Venezuela' or 'Hugo Chávez' in the index of either book. Sunkara focuses very little on Latin America, except to briefly introduce the Pink Tide movement (Sunkara 2019, p. 156). Robinson briefly mentions Venezuela as a bad example of socialism (Robinson 2019, pp. 15-16).

[110] Luis Beltrán Prieto was one of the few left-wing populist leaders who managed to break through the system to gain some share in power.

other nations. The term thereby references U.S. interests rather than conditions in the target nation. In Venezuela, 'stability' amounts to preserving the basic power structure of the nation and the political parties and institutions supporting that power structure. The system, then, greatly benefited the major players in that system. In exchange for protecting capital, civil society, and the Venezuelan economy, it offered the appearance of legitimacy. Predictably, this system didn't benefit most ordinary Venezuelans. Their standard of living remained low.

For the U.S. left, this is one of the most important lessons about foreign policy jargon. Experts, pundits, and politicians use the word 'stability' freely in their discussion of other nations. It's important for leftists to understand what that word means. It refers to the maintenance of U.S. interests rather than the interests of ordinary people in other nations. In fact, the term is perfectly compatible with mass *instability* for the ordinary people who live in the target nation. The term stands out as one of the most misleading ones in foreign policy discussions. Everyone in U.S. politics agrees that 'stability' is good. But leftists should always ask, "stability for whom?"

Corruption escalated in Venezuela over time, getting noticeably worse after a late 1980s economic recession[111]. President Carlos Andrés Pérez compounded these problems by accepting International Monetary Fund (IMF) loan money. The IMF attached austerity conditions to the money, conditions imposing decreased social spending by the Venezuelan government and resulting in increased poverty and mass protests. All these events violated the basic deal behind the Puntofijo Pact, triggering mass unrest and coup attempts. Pérez survived multiple such attempts – including one led by Hugo Chávez himself – but he was impeached in 1993. This left the Puntofijo Pact and the entire Venezuelan democratic system ripe for collapse. Collapse then materialized in 1993 with the election of Rafael Caldera.

---

[111] More broadly, the late 1980s recession is the point at which some analysts date the beginnings of the rumblings that brought Chávez to power. See, for example, Gonzalez 2018, especially p. 30.

Caldera won at the head of a 'National Convergence' rather than as a member of a major political party. More an *ad hoc* coalition than political party, his 'convergence' ran from center-right to Marxist left. By winning with this coalition, Caldera weakened Venezuela's major political forces. However, his coalition was unwieldy. He'd likely never have made it work, but conditions took away the opportunity to even try. A new recession, banking crisis, and more IMF loans and austerity ended all hope. Far from an answer to the problems, Caldera's convergence was an ill-fated attempt to put the old and the new together in a broad coalition. Venezuelans didn't like what had come before, but no one offered a solid vision for next steps.

Hugo Chávez swept to power in 1998 with more than 56% of the vote, offering Venezuelans precisely this missing vision. He organized a coalition called the Fifth Republic Movement (Movimiento Quinta República) around a new constitution and new system. Chávez made no pretense of working within the old order, and most Venezuelans loved him for it. It formed the core of his appeal. He built the movement around three goals: writing a new constitution, ending poverty, and fighting corruption. None of these goals were unique to Latin American populist politics. But, unlike many others, Chávez worked hard to accomplish them. Let's look at each in turn.

First, almost immediately after taking office Chávez created a constituent national assembly to write a new constitution. Both the process and outcome were unusually democratic and participatory. The new constitution established: Indigenous political representation, restrictions on non-Indigenous patenting of Indigenous knowledge, protections for women, and broad public rights – from education to food, health care, and housing. It added new environmental protections and included ways to oversee and recall government officials. That's the positive. It also dramatically strengthened the office of the presidency. It lengthened terms and term limits and gave the president various means of working around the legislature. That's less positive. And it did all these things – positive and negative – at the same time. This formed a frequent theme of the Chávez administration and a force behind both his successes and failures. He combined a stronger presidency with more popular participation, largely at the expense of legislators and lobbyists. He also made bold moves, such as renaming the country the Bolivarian Republic of Venezuela. This made him popular, but it also made him a target. And it increased the country's reliance on his personal power, enabling the U.S. and Venezuelan elite to undermine his administration more effectively. Thus, Chávez was neither dictator nor democrat. He offered neither a fully participatory system nor an authoritarian regime.

Second, Chávez delivered on his promise to fight poverty. Overall, poverty dropped from 43% in 1999 to 27% in 2012[112], but even this understates the dramatic nature of the decline. Poverty briefly *rose* during an early coup attempt in 2002-2003. This means Chávez cut poverty in half in only 4 years – 2003 to 2007. We see a similar pattern with extreme poverty, rising from 18% in 1999 to 30% in 2003, and then all the way down to 8% by 2012. Dramatic poverty reduction bought him a great deal of goodwill and mandate to govern. In addition to direct poverty reduction, Chávez provided support to those who remained in poverty. He created an array of social programs for this latter task. His Bolivarian Missions tackled a wide range of issues, and they did so with historic levels of public funding. This social democratic governance massively uplifted Venezuela's underclass in a way never seen in the country and only rarely seen anywhere in the world.

Chávez's record on the third issue – corruption – was mixed. The Venezuelan opposition to Chávez – and its American allies – frequently cited corruption as the basis for their objections. And this did have *some* basis in reality. The Bolivarian project – at a broad level – combined social democracy with class collaboration. The social democracy component was often participatory. Chávez built communal councils to make democratic decisions at the local level. These were highly participatory organizations that side-stepped corrupt local officials[113]. However, the class collaboration component often retained and expanded corruption. Chávez

---

[112] See these useful charts from the Center for Strategic and International Studies: https://www.csis.org/analysis/venezuelan-drama-14-charts. Last accessed July 29, 2020.

[113] Readers might be interested in comparing the Venezuelan communal councils to local movements constitutionally authorized to act in other South American nations. For an overview of the experience in Ecuador, see Riofrancos 2020, pp. 117-119.

established patron-client relationships with private capital – especially leaders of domestic industry. Corruption thereby expanded, especially within the state-owned oil and natural gas company, PDVSA. The domestic Venezuelan left – from anarchists to communists[114] – heavily criticized Chávez on these grounds. Chávez had his reasons for doing some of these things, particularly the 2002-2004 coup attempts we'll examine in the next section. But these facts do not excuse Chávez's conflicts with workers. He often didn't take workers' side in clashes with favored officials of domestic industry and the state.

The big picture? Chávez's social democratic program made solid gains through at least 2009. He steadily progressed toward his three goals, sweeping away the old regime, sharply reducing poverty, and fighting (some) corruption. He used the tools of progressive taxation, wealth transfer, and government programs to improve lives. His coalition promoted popular involvement in politics, though always in line with its own power. Chávez was far less successful in turning the Bolivarian program into a fully socialist one. The communal councils never defeated domestic capital and its political allies. The system always depended on them. Attempts to diversify and democratize the economy by creating a social economy showed promising results, but it never moved the country beyond its oil economy[115]. From co-op businesses to worker-owned factories, et al. – most projects failed due to political patronage, mismanagement, or lack of funding and support.

Major gains didn't last long after Chávez's death. U.S. intervention accounted for *some* of this, as we'll see later. But it didn't account for *all* of it. Other major factors included: lack of economic diversification, too much centralized authority, and strong opposition from domestic elites. Chávez's successor – Nicolás Maduro – has succeeded in holding on to power for almost a decade. But that's close to the full list of his successes.

---

[114] There are many domestic Venezuelan leftist organizations that have criticized the Bolivarian project to a greater or lesser degree. But some of the more interesting lines of criticism come from Marea Socialista, a largely Trotskyist group that opposes both the current Maduro Administration and the Venezuelan opposition. The group instead tends to unite with Indigenous political forces.

[115] See Wilpert 2007 for an overview of Venezuela's use of the social economy.

He won a (likely fair) election in 2013 and a (likely much less fair) election in 2018. No political coalition emerged that could take power from the remnants of the Chávez coalition. And so, Maduro remains as a major force. But most gains from the early 2000s have been wiped out and then some. Poverty started sharply rising in 2014 and never quit rising. The last thing approaching a reliable measure pointed to an 87% poverty rate in 2017, double the rate when Chávez first took office. Since 2017, all we know for sure is that there's a small group of elites who aren't poor. Almost everyone else is poor. Venezuela suffers from: shortages of food and other basic necessities, runaway inflation[116], massive cuts to social spending, and multiple coup attempts. The stats are real, *not* a fabrication of any propaganda machine. Broad sources – sometimes even the Maduro administration itself – confirm them.

In short, the Maduro administration isn't a successful experiment in socialist governance. Far from it. Whether through U.S. meddling, bad domestic management, or economic forces, the once promising Chávez administration has turned into a disappointment, embarrassment, or failed state. Where one lands among these explanations tends to match where one lands on the Ciccariello-Maher/Livingstone to Robinson/Sunkara spectrum. We have some work to do to sort out the story.

U.S. Intervention in Venezuela: Two Waves

The U.S. intervenes in Venezuela in many ways. But I'll highlight two major waves in the last 20 years. This provides us with a useful way to divide up the lessons. The first wave came during the early years of the Chávez administration from about 2002 to 2004. The second began shortly after Maduro's election, and it continues to the present. The U.S. still intervened between these two periods – particularly during the 2006 and 2012 election cycles – but these two waves offer us clear and insightful cases.

---

[116] Readers looking for documentation of these phenomena should begin with the sources in these respective Wikipedia articles: https://en.wikipedia.org/wiki/Shortages_in_Venezuela; https://en.wikipedia.org/wiki/Hyperinflation_in_Venezuela. Last accessed July 29, 2020.

The first wave centered on the 2002-2003 coup attempt against Chávez. In theory, domestic forces drove the events. These forces include Chávez's allegedly anti-democratic practices – particularly his use of an enabling law to rule by decree – his attempts at sidelining the legislature, and his moves against the private news media. In practice, opponents disliked Chávez's assertion of state ownership of PDVSA, his land reform proposals, and his directing of state funds to popular groups. The coup emanated from business leaders united with certain elements of the Venezuelan military. It gained some level of popular support from the Confederación de Trabajadores de Venezuela (CTV), a mainstream labor federation affiliated with the Democratic Action Party. These elements were heavily invested in the old, pre-Chávez (and even pre-Caldera) political system. When Chávez swept away the old order, he swept away their political power. They wanted it back.

The coup removed Chávez from power for about 2 days, replacing him with Pedro Carmona. Carmona originally made his money in the petrochemical industry. At the time of the coup, however, he was the leader of Fedecámaras, a business federation. Clearly representing Venezuelan capital rather than its people, Carmona had little popular support and no history of popular leadership. The vast majority of the military and public remained loyal to Chávez, enabling him to return to power practically overnight. The coup, therefore, quickly failed. While it left a lasting impact on state security, it didn't change the system.

We know the U.S. played a role in these events, but the nature of that role remains unclear. Multiple U.S. foreign aid programs and civic groups – notably the National Endowment for Democracy (NED) and the AFL-CIO's Solidarity Center[117] – funded the CTV. This is, of course, without mentioning the United States Agency for International Development (USAID). USAID had an even heavier hand in promoting the shared interests of U.S. and Venezuelan capital. The U.S. frequently operates through groups with seemingly innocuous or even positive names that have very non-innocuous and negative functions. We should recall here

---

[117] For a recent overview of NED spending on Venezuela, see: https://www.ned.org/region/latin-america-and-caribbean/venezuela-2018/. Last accessed: July 29, 2020.

Jessica Trisko Darden's point – which we examined in Chapter 2 – that even apparently well-intentioned aid funds violence. The Solidarity Center has long worked toward anti-communist and other anti-leftist goals in the mainstream labor movement. And much of its funding comes from U.S. state agencies promoting similar aims[118]. It consistently promotes U.S. interests in other nations over and above the interests of those people themselves. The NED serves similar purposes as a state agency. It claims to promote civil society, democracy, and human rights around the globe. In fact, it promotes these things only when in line with perceived U.S. interests.

Chávez asserted that the U.S. played a more expansive role. In fact, the evidence for the claim is mixed. He asserted that the U.S. knew about and approved the plans – even that U.S. military officers were present in the country at the time of the coup. We don't know for sure the accuracy of these claims. It was clearly in Chavez's interests to exaggerate U.S. direct involvement in order to unite Venezuelans against a common enemy. And so, we ought to take these assertions with a grain of salt. In support, however, the New York Times reported on C.I.A. documents showing at least some prior knowledge of the coup within the U.S. intelligence community[119]. Explicitly pro-Chávez activist Eva Golinger used some of these sources to assert direct U.S. involvement in – perhaps even leadership of – the coup in her 2006 book *The Chavez Code*[120]. But Golinger arguably stretches the available evidence, and she rather uncritically supports the 1999-2013 administration. We do know coup leaders thought the U.S. would approve of their actions, especially given U.S. support for similar actions elsewhere. The U.S. routinely supports coups where governments make capital nervous. The U.S. therefore exerted a strong indirect influence even if not a direct one.

The coup's failure left Venezuelan capital in a difficult position. It had the much less attractive option of winning a recall election against Chávez

---

[118] For a representative sample of its funding, see: https://www.solidaritycenter.org/wp-content/uploads/2014/11/Annual-Report.2013.pdf. Last accessed July 29, 2020.
[119] See: https://www.nytimes.com/2004/12/03/washington/world/documents-show-cia-knew-of-a-coup-plot-in-venezuela.html. Last accessed: July 29, 2020.
[120] Golinger 2005.

in 2004 – an option ironically provided by the rewritten constitution itself. This went about as badly for the opposition as one might expect. Chávez won 59% of the vote – even greater than his 1998 majority, thus demonstrating Chávez's power and popular support. And, of course, the U.S. funded the recall effort. It provided NED grants to Súmate, the organization collecting signatures for the recall efforts[121]. This merely compounded the failures of Venezuelan capital and its U.S. allies.

The second wave began much later, after Chávez's death and Maduro's ascension to power. It centers on the current economic crisis. The U.S. criticized the 2013 election results, proceeding gradually to supporting new coup attempts. In particular, it heavily backed the failed 2019 coup of Juan Guaidó. Unlike Carmona, Guaidó had an electoral base. He also led a political party – the Popular Will Party – that isn't an *obvious* vehicle for the interests of capital, even describing itself as 'progressive' and 'social democratic.' Its brand of social democracy remains very friendly to capital, but it wasn't an obvious non-starter. It's genuine to the extent that it reflects political change in a country after 20 years of leftist rule. Venezuelans don't want to go back to what came before, and even right-wing parties must adjust to this new reality. However, Guaidó's approval ratings are abysmal[122]. He quickly fell out of favor with everyone other than his own inner circle, and Venezuelans know him as a feckless coup-plotter.

To some extent, we see the same old players. The Solidarity Center again received almost $10 million from the U.S. government. This included funding from the NED[123]. We don't yet know whether that money is going directly to the CTV and/or to coup activities, but it's highly likely. Furthermore, by 2019 the U.S. government made little pretense of sending its aid for humanitarian purposes. It shifted aid from the larger USAID program to deliver directly to Guaidó's phony

---

[121] See Human Rights Watch: https://www.hrw.org/news/2005/07/07/venezuela-court-orders-trial-civil-society-leaders. Last accessed: July 29, 2020.

[122] See: https://en.wikipedia.org/wiki/Juan_Guaid%C3%B3#Polls. Last accessed: July 29, 2020. Despite this, as of early 2021, the Biden Administration still backs him.

[123] See: https://afgj.org/what-is-the-afl-cios-solidarity-center-doing-in-venezuela-we-have-a-right-to-know. Last accessed: July 29, 2020.

'government[124].' But we also see new players. In one of the stranger events in Venezuelan history, a U.S. military veteran named Jordan Gondreau – head of the security company Silvercorp USA – organized a failed uprising. In fact, Venezuelan fishermen sympathetic to the Maduro administration captured the would-be coup-plotters. The U.S. government, of course, denied any involvement. But people in U.S. military circles are certainly still interested in violent uprising in the region[125].

Why is There a Crisis in Venezuela?

We find as many explanations for the current crisis as we find explainers. Many explanations serve the people offering them. Venezuelan elites cite capital flight[126]. They blame Maduro's corruption and bad management. Maduro cites economic sabotage and blames U.S. and Venezuelan elites. Some elements of the left cite both[127].

The two sides tell a partial truth, as we've seen above. The Venezuelan opposition – backed by the U.S. – *does* engage in economic sabotage in numerous ways. It focused on these methods during the 2002-2003 coup attempt and the 2004 recall referendum. Sharply rising poverty rates resulted from these efforts. However, sabotage didn't dislodge the close bond between Chávez and Venezuela's poor. Undermining the economy *could* have dislodged the close bond between Chávez and Venezuela's poor. But much like Pedro Carmona and domestic capital, Juan Guaidó and his allies lack a broad base of support. It's hardly a stretch to imagine the same playbook at work in newer movements against Maduro. After

---

[124]https://www.thenation.com/article/archive/venezuela-washington-funded-counterrevolution/; https://www.ft.com/content/a739edb4-a8ed-11e9-984c-fac8325aaa04. Last accessed: July 29, 2020.

[125] See: https://www.cnbc.com/2020/05/05/us-veteran-behind-failed-venezuela-plot-says-american-mercenaries-detained.html; https://www.bellingcat.com/news/2020/05/05/the-invasion-of-venezuela-brought-to-you-by-silvercorp-usa/. Last accessed: July 29, 2020.

[126] By this, they mean that capital 'flew' from the country when investors withdrew funds and infrastructure.

[127] See: https://www.thenation.com/article/archive/why-is-venezuela-in-crisis/. Last accessed: July 29, 2020.

all, these new actors hold largely the same interests and motivations. An increasingly desperate coup movement might find sabotage attractive.

However, Chávez and later Maduro held a wide variety of tools to prevent these actions and/or mitigate their effects. They largely failed to do so. Diversifying the economy and bringing it under much greater democratic ownership and control would've helped. Neither leader succeeded in doing so. Instead they strengthened domestic capital in the pursuit of social democracy via class collaboration. Furthermore, by yielding too much power to the presidency under its new constitution, Venezuela couldn't recover from the death of Chávez. Maduro simply didn't have the political skills to maintain the Chávez coalition. Even at his most effective, he remains weaker than Chávez, leaving him able to remain in office but accomplishing little. Finally, Venezuela maintains layer upon layer of corruption. The patron-client system under Chávez and Maduro stands out. Any look at the deeper causes of the current crisis must account for these factors.

So, what *were* the causes of the current crisis? Instability in oil prices – notably the sharp drop in oil prices starting in 2014 and continuing to the present day – emerge as the largest direct cause[128]. The domestic Venezuelan left and even international press recognize this. Venezuela never diversified its economy or adequately built a social economy. It failed to break free of its dependence on revenue from energy rents, and thus it couldn't institute the kinds of structural economic changes it needed. Nor did it successfully build the kind of open, democratic, participatory politics it needed to build its social economy[129]. As a result, it still relies heavily on oil to maintain social democratic programs. Any disruption to the oil economy – even a fairly minor one – presented a threat. A major disruption of the sort they actually faced presented nothing short of catastrophe.

---

[128] For an overview, see: https://en.wikipedia.org/wiki/2010s_oil_glut. Last accessed: July 29, 2020.

[129] See Gonzalez 2018, especially pp. 115-119 for a history of this problem. Gonzalez points out that while Maduro stamped out popular movements, Chávez himself never adequately supported those movements. He especially moved away from those movements after the creation of the PSUV. See also Riofrancos 2020, especially pp. 170-172.

Of course, to pin the blame on oil prices is merely to move the debate between Maduro and his opponents one step back. Maduro gladly attributes the drop of oil prices to U.S. interference and coercion. And the Venezuelan opposition and U.S. press gladly attribute it to normal economic forces and capital flight. Once again, the truth is more complicated than either side allows. The U.S. sharply increased oil production in and around the 2008 Global Recession. Why? Did it set its sights on economic recovery, or on undermining nations deeply embedded within the oil economy? It probably aimed at doing both. The U.S. tried to reduce its dependence on fossil fuels due to both the climate crisis and the slowdown in the Chinese economy. That's one example. And so, the U.S. partially caused these events, but not necessarily on purpose. Maybe it aimed these moves at Venezuela, or maybe the impact on Venezuela was only a side effect. The U.S. operated with complex motives.

We find, then, many 'normal' economic forces, rivalries, and moves by world powers. But other signs point to the kinds of nefarious causes Maduro likes to cite. Internal OPEC rivalries – especially any associated with Saudi actions – surely helped along the drop in oil prices. Saudi rulers pushed for greater oil production, and more production dropped prices. The Saudis, of course, are heavily funded and supported by the U.S. The U.S. uses them as a key ally in oil-producing regions and often as a proxy for U.S. interests. Even if the U.S. didn't directly stand behind Saudi efforts, it almost certainly encouraged those efforts.

We have, then, a 'perfect storm' as the cause. How did we get a crisis in Venezuela? Many things came together. This includes: Maduro's corruption and poor management, Venezuela's dependence on the oil economy and lack of economic diversification, the political system's dependence on the personality of Hugo Chávez, and efforts on the part of the Venezuelan opposition – often aided by the United States and always aided by multiple elements of domestic Venezuelan capital – in exploiting these factors to weaken the Maduro government and restore the country to rule by capital. Bring these things together and you end up with 87+% poverty rates.

Venezuela and the Four Basic Principles

How can we use our four basic principles to critique and improve U.S. policy in Venezuela? One clear lesson for U.S. leftists is that we must avoid conflating our own intentions with the intentions of the country as a whole. When Venezuelan leaders subvert democracy in the name of socialism, this upsets leftists. And rightly so. We rightly believe that socialism is democratic, open, and transparent. When its proponents set these things aside, we find it to be a big problem. This tempts some leftists to argue that 'we' – the 'we' of the U.S. as a whole, represented in the form of the state – should oppose Maduro and support opposition-led civil society movements. The trouble here is that the U.S. government is *no ally* in this kind of struggle. The 'we' we think we refer to simply *doesn't exist*. The U.S. left has to build it through careful, long struggle. U.S. intervention in the present environment creates a worse situation. Advocating for state intervention in Venezuela should therefore be off the table at the outset. The U.S. funds 'democracy' and 'civil society' in Venezuela. It does so through groups like the NED and USAID. But these organizations promote a false 'democracy' that the U.S. left doesn't want. We want genuine democracy. And so, the left must look for a different path to promote democracy in Venezuela.

Nevertheless, leftists want to do *something* to stand in solidarity with Venezuelans. That's noble and worthwhile. If not U.S. government funding, then *what*? The left must build its own bonds of solidarity with allies among the domestic Venezuelan left. It needs to create direct links between American leftists and Venezuelan leftists. How do we do this? One option is to attend or support some of the events organized by the Venezuelan state itself. Chávez widely organized and promoted these events, and Maduro still does on occasion. Maduro, for example, organized an International Encounter against Imperialism, for Peace, Sovereignty, and Life[130] in 2020. These events directly connect Americans and Venezuelans, and they provide a forum for support. For this reason, leftists should put it on the table as an option. But we should sound a cautionary note. These events often include support for very problematic

---

[130] See: https://venezuelanalysis.com/images/14776. Last accessed: July 29, 2020.

– and very non-leftist – regimes, such as the al-Assad regime in Syria. It's easy for Maduro – and far worse governments than the one in Venezuela – to use these events for propaganda purposes. And so, the left must draw a clear line between opposition to U.S. intervention in a nation and outright endorsement of that nation's practices. This becomes especially relevant when those practices aren't ones the left wants to encourage. Leaning in too hard to events sponsored by the Venezuelan government threatens to blur that line.

A second – and preferable – option is to create direct, organic links with democratic and leftist groups without mediation from the state. But to do this, the left has to *organize*, especially up front. Good organizing and the organic links that result will deepen our conversations and greatly broaden the range of our potential accomplishments. As Jane McAlevey would put it[131] – in the realm of labor organizing, but directly applicable here – there are simply no shortcuts to doing good international solidarity work. This work proceeds best with direct links between U.S. and Venezuelan working-class and leftist movements. Only through these direct links will we help Venezuela while learning lessons we can apply to our domestic movements.

There are many ways to organize organic links with Venezuelans. All of them run through connecting with Venezuelan workers and workers' organizations. And they run through connecting with these groups without the mediation of officials directly tied to Maduro or his administration. One option is to build bridges with the communal councils, at least any of them still in operation. Another option is to build links with the Venezuelan trade union movement, particularly the left wing of that movement. A third possibility is connecting with leftist political parties not directly tied to Maduro's United Socialist Party of Venezuela (PSUV). But this third option holds less attraction. It's particularly challenging, and the left might not want to oppose the PSUV in all its aspects. Hands Off Venezuela in the U.K. runs through direct links with Venezuelan trade unions as a key part of its mission. But I can't speak to whether – or to what degree – the group has succeeded in its

---

[131] McAlevey 2018.

mission[132]. One key challenge the left faces is the need to balance criticism of the state with the need to maintain good relations with workers who often back the state. All these things stand out as starting points worth considering[133].

The U.S. left can and should directly apply the principle of non-interventionism. It's imperative that we oppose U.S. intervention in Venezuela. We find few – if any – cases of the U.S. acting in its official capacity as a force for good from a leftist perspective. It causes great harm in the nation and would likely do so even if the U.S. elected a progressive president in the near future. I'll allow that we do find certain cases of humanitarian need where the U.S. can intervene without doing harm. But we don't find cases like that when the U.S. shows open hostility toward the nation. Venezuela provides us with a good case for why non-interventionism applies not only to extreme cases like the War in Iraq, but also more broadly to cases where the U.S.'s infamous 'democracy promotion' machine springs into action. These things rarely go well. And even when they do, they promote U.S. interests over and above the interests of Venezuelans.

Gabriel Hetland argues similarly in a 2019 Jacobin article, "Venezuela and the Left[134]." While Hetland appeals to non-interventionism, he bolsters it with twin appeals to self-determination and solidarity. He thinks – in short – that Venezuelans must collectively and democratically work their own way out of recent events. And he thinks that the U.S should stay out of it. Hetland finds it a complicated case because of Maduro's role in causing the current problems – as we saw earlier in detail. But he argues that awareness and support for the Venezuelan left – while maintaining an official hands-off attitude – best serves leftists in both nations. He advocates this hands-off attitude both at the level of the U.S. government and at the level of individual leftists and leftist groups. I think Hetland is correct on non-interventionism, but he doesn't go far enough

---

[132] See: https://www.handsoffvenezuela.org/about-us.htm. Last accessed June 5, 2020.

[133] We might again consider the discussion of the Central American Solidarity Movement found in Striffler 2019 and referenced earlier in Chapter 2.

[134] See: https://www.jacobinmag.com/2019/02/venezuela-noninterventionism-self-determination-solidarity. Last accessed: July 29, 2020.

on positive actions the left can take. Done well, the bonds of international solidarity we develop could help the left move beyond *mere* non-interventionism. We could move into the realm of promoting a democratic, international, *pluralistic* order. Many immigrants still arrive from Venezuela to the U.S. Promoting international links carries the potential to better integrate Venezuelan immigrants into U.S. unions and the U.S. labor movement. And so, while international solidarity and non-interventionism are the principles most applicable to Venezuela, pluralism has its uses.

Promoting these principles will help give Venezuela space. Due to its recent failures, Venezuela is no longer at the cutting edge of anti-capitalist alternatives and anti-hegemony action. But it could get there again in the future. We see, then, that these first three principles – interpreted and applied well – come together to create a much larger whole. They create much stronger movements. We'll return to the fourth principle after discussing Bolivia. Workers' movements are stronger with Venezuelans as participants.

Bolivia, Settler-Colonialism, and Native Americans

Before finishing our discussion of Latin America, we'll take a brief look at a second example. The situation in Bolivia offers us ways to enrich our discussion. Bolivia has fewer people and it's less entangled with the oil economy. It offers the U.S. fewer obvious reasons to intervene. As a result, Bolivia had a bit more space than Venezuela to develop anti-capitalist politics over the same time period[135]. Nevertheless, the U.S. still intervenes to a certain degree. And Bolivian capital – as well as dominant racial interests, as we'll see – has left its mark on the nation. For these reasons, we have special challenges in thinking and writing about Bolivia

---

[135] But there's a deeper question over whether it *did*. See Veltmeyer and Petras 2014 for several essays – the introduction and the chapter specifically on Bolivia – arguing that Bolivia largely failed to do so. The basic line here is that while Bolivia might have had more space than Venezuela, it was less committed to an anti-capitalist approach. Specifically, the essays argue that Bolivia did not reduce dependence on foreign direct investment from capital to nearly the degree that Venezuela did. See also Gonzalez 2018 for a largely confirming perspective. Gonzalez points out that the greater balances of power in Bolivia were largely between Morales and the business classes, where he largely left popular movements behind (pp. 75-78).

from a U.S. policy perspective. Most of the forces at work in Bolivia are internal to the nation itself, and they descend from a deep colonial legacy. We'll keep this background in mind as we work through the situation.

We need a settler-colonialism frame to understand much of the backdrop to Bolivian politics. Settler-colonialism forms a deep part of Bolivian history, and that history exerts a continuing influence. We might well argue it's the single largest factor in explaining Bolivian society and divisions in its political system. Newer leftists might not be fully familiar with the idea of settler-colonialism. In the U.S., identity-based groups are as likely as leftist groups to use the term. And these groups often use the term much more broadly and expansively than the term ought to be used. It's a simple enough term, roughly combining the concepts of 'settlement' and 'colonialism.' Empires travel to a new place to bring that place under its domination, i.e., colonialism. What distinguishes settler-colonialism from other forms is that the empire brings with it a group of people to *displace* the native population of the colonized territory[136]. For people in the U.S., the displacement of Native Americans from the U.S. Midwest and West – and accompanying white homesteader settlement of these areas – stands out as the obvious example.

Bolivia stands out because it still has a large Indigenous population, even after the impact of settler-colonialism. It has the largest and most diverse Native American population in the Western Hemisphere. In fact, it easily holds this title, with about 20% of Bolivia's population living in Indigenous communities. Community members come from dozens of different ethnic groups, making Bolivia one of the most diverse nations in the world. These communities divide between highland and lowland parts of the country, and we could draw further distinctions. Including people with mixed European and Indigenous ancestry – a significant portion of the population anywhere in Latin America, but particularly in Bolivia – Indigenous people easily make up a majority of the nation's population.

---

[136] This is another of the rare circumstances where Wikipedia proves surprisingly useful as an introductory tool for readers. See: https://en.wikipedia.org/wiki/Settler_colonialism. Last accessed June 5, 2020.

Nevertheless, the interests of the white European minority dominated Bolivia from its early 19th century independence until the 2005 election. They did so despite countless waves of revolution and highly skilled organizing work by Indigenous Bolivians. The Bolivian state assumed many forms during this nearly 200-year period. It passed through phases of liberal democracy, military dictatorship, and variations on these themes. But through it all, whites dominated the nation and its resources. They did so through their own set of complicated maneuvers. For one example, consider Gonzalo Sánchez de Lozada, the president prior to Evo Morales. He took certain steps toward popular nationalism. For one, he joined the Revolutionary National Movement (Movimiento Nacionalista Revolucionario), a historically leftist and nationalist political force in Bolivia. But he was in fact a U.S.-educated fiscal conservative who many Bolivians outright nicknamed 'El Gringo.' The nickname was especially popular among Bolivia's Indigenous communities. Sánchez de Lozada resigned the presidency and fled to the U.S. in 2003. He did so for reasons similar to those that toppled Caldera in Venezuela. Evo Morales's Indigenous popular movement gained traction in Bolivia like no other, for reasons we'll see below.

Evo Morales and the Movement for Socialism

Bolivia elected Evo Morales in 2005 as the nation's first Indigenous president. He won at the head of the Movement for Socialism (MAS) political party. MAS received an absolute majority of the vote in a multi-party election. Morales achieved victory at the head of a coalition built around a union between Indigenous interests and the interests of Bolivia's poorer classes. But building a successful electoral campaign around Indigenous support was a first in Bolivia. And it turned out to be no fluke. Morales expanded his coalition in the 2009 election, winning 64% of the vote. His vote share remained above 60% as late as 2014. Like the Chávez movement in Venezuela, MAS remains the only political force in Bolivia capable of putting together a political majority. The current situation in

Bolivia leaves its coalition as the only group sufficiently broad to achieve a popular mandate[137].

Morales himself comes from the Indigenous Aymara community in the Bolivian Andes highlands. He built his activism on the interests of farmers in his home region, particularly coca growers. Coca growers long suffered under pressure from the U.S. and from Bolivian capital. The war on drugs – and the coca growers' role in the drug trade – loomed large over the conflict between growers, capital, and the U.S. military. This conflict thrust Morales and MAS to the very front of U.S. policy in Bolivia. It created for them both political dangers and potential power. Readers presumably know the dangers all too well, but the potential for power always existed alongside those dangers. Morales's activism put him in a place of potential influence, with a movement that existed at a key pressure point in the economy and foreign relations. MAS needed only a key event to unite the interests of coca growers with those of other parts of the Bolivian working classes.

This event arrived in the form of a conflict over the use of Bolivia's natural gas reserves[138]. While the oil economy isn't as central in Bolivia as in Venezuela, natural gas plays a large role in the Bolivian economy. On its face, the conflict was about extraction policy and the use of Bolivia's natural resources. But deeper issues simmered under the surface. The conflict deeply involved a wide range of Indigenous Bolivians from both the highlands and the lowlands. Any conflict uniting the interests of coca growers with other marginalized groups carried strong potential to bring a shock to the Bolivian system. And Morales had already performed this task at a smaller scale. He had united coca growers and put them together as a cohesive Indigenous political unit. The natural gas conflict allowed him to expand this group even further. By this point, the alliance grew so large it constituted a potential political majority.

---

[137] This is hardly a hypothetical, given that MAS *did* achieve a popular mandate via electoral majority in Bolivia's 2020 election.
[138]https://web.archive.org/web/20060630181559/http://www.zmag.org/content/showarticle.cfm?SectionID=52&ItemID=10202;
https://www.nzherald.co.nz/business/news/article.cfm?c_id=3&objectid=10379942;
http://news.bbc.co.uk/2/hi/americas/4963348.stm. Last accessed: July 29, 2020.

And so, the natural gas conflict put Morales and MAS in an excellent position. With the right campaign, they could seize formal political control of the country. They did so in 2005, uniting coca growers with a broad coalition of marginalized Bolivians to take a huge electoral win. Political forces similar to those in Venezuela had discredited Bolivia's political establishment. This background further expanded the size of the MAS majority. Early opposition to Morales was isolated to narrow, powerful economic and political elites. They could make trouble for Morales, and indeed they did. They built a local autonomy movement almost the minute Morales took office, and that movement tried to sabotage him. But by winning more than 60% at the polls, Morales unmasked his opposition, uncovering their elite economic interests and making it clear how those interests drove their political views. As a result, Morales kept them to about one-third of the national popular vote.

What did Morales do in office? We again find useful comparisons to Venezuela. He increased social spending along social democratic lines. This built a base of support among poor and otherwise marginalized people around promotion of their interests and advancement. And we find economic data similar to those in Venezuela[139]. MAS reduced extreme poverty by half, and it doubled the country's GDP in under a decade. Morales rolled back the nation's colonized economy. He did so by increasing the state sector and moving to a mixed economic system. Bolivian companies and the Bolivian people shared the profits and benefits from resources. This general trend culminated in an ambitious plan to nationalize Bolivia's electrical grid.

U.S. policy toward Bolivia in the early years should be familiar to us, if a bit subdued compared to Venezuela. Morales frequently accused the U.S. of using USAID money to foment unrest. The U.S. encouraged and inflamed the local autonomy movement run by Bolivian elites, doing so as a part of its anti-drug, counter-narcotics efforts. These things simmered as a source of tension with a president and movement centered on coca growers. Morales himself took a mixed and complicated attitude toward

---

[139] https://www.npr.org/sections/goatsandsoda/2019/11/26/781199250/how-evo-morales-made-bolivia-a-better-place-before-he-was-forced-to-flee. Last accessed: October 26, 2020.

U.S. anti-drug policy. He used the coca plant as a symbol of anti-imperialist resistance, which stood out as the obvious move. But at the same time he also selectively accepted and utilized U.S. foreign aid around anti-drug programs[140]. This leaves U.S. leftists with much to work through. We sit with thorny complexities when considering analysis and possible bonds of international solidarity.

2019 Coup and Aftermath

Evo Morales won the 2019 Bolivian election. But he dropped to under 50% of the vote, and he's no longer the president of the country. What happened? Here's a narrow and legalistic answer. Morales resigned the presidency in November 2019. Shortly afterward, his legal successor, Adriana Salvatierra of the Movement for Socialism, also resigned. The next person in line was a right-wing opposition leader, Jeanine Áñez. She took charge of the nation. Those are the basic facts. But – in truth – even these basic facts remain in dispute. Technically, the Bolivian Senate did not accept Salvatierra's resignation before naming her replacement. This leaves the issue of Bolivia's 'rightful' president at the time something of a tossup between Salvatierra and Áñez. Legal or not, the facts on the ground placed Áñez in charge. Predictably, the U.S. firmly allied itself with Áñez[141].

Here's a more informative answer. Morales – and then Salvatierra – resigned in November 2019 in the face of mass protests. The events remain in dispute, questionable enough for us to fairly label the entire series of events a 'coup.' It wasn't an obvious coup, but it was a softer one. Protesters aligned themselves with the displaced economic and political elite, but they expanded well beyond the elite. Protests took off over the (probably false) allegations of electoral fraud in 2019 and (probably true) allegations that Morales subverted the democratic system by standing for

---

[140] See: https://www.nytimes.com/2008/08/29/world/americas/29bolivia.html. Last accessed June 5, 2020.

[141] And potentially more than this. In January 2020, Donald Trump signed a White House memorandum that would unlock a wider range of U.S. aid to the new Bolivian regime. See https://www.whitehouse.gov/presidential-actions/presidential-determination-waiving-restriction-united-states-assistance-bolivia/. Last accessed June 5, 2020.

a new term in the 2019 election. And so, protests combined political opportunism by Bolivian elites with real dissent and problems within Bolivian leftist politics. But the protests turned heavily in Morales's favor after the coup. However, by that point the damage had been done. While it's true that Morales's MAS coalition won the next election in 2020, it begins governance anew by looking arguably weaker and more vulnerable than during the Morales years. It will be forced to find new paths to power and governance.

I think all this provides the U.S. left with a number of important lessons. First, representation alone isn't enough. Morales represented a range of marginalized groups, and he represented them well. Bolivia's Indigenous population suffered under decades – centuries – of white, colonial domination. But this does not absolve the leader of all fault. Readers need only consider the case of Robert Mugabe in Zimbabwe to reinforce this point. Morales never adequately planned for a successor to his MAS movement. Much like Chávez in Venezuela, he had little apparent future plan. What would happen at the end of his term? There seemed to be nothing in mind, and lack of planning drove Morales to subvert the constitution. When his own referendum to modify that constitution failed, he searched for less legitimate ways to remain in office. This string of failures traces to a problem common to Bolivia and Venezuela – excessive reliance on a leader and on the office of the presidency. None of this is to pin all the blame on Morales. Perhaps there are local issues on the ground that made it difficult to name a successor. But the lesson for the left stands out. We should always do what we can to promote democratic inclusion and mass participation.

Second, even when the left defeats elites, these elites maintain spheres of influence and alliances with global capital. Global capital never quit financing Bolivian elites, even if it did so more quietly than in Venezuela. Elites organized a local autonomy movement. They did so during a time when they won but a small fraction of the vote nationwide. MAS exposed the Bolivian opposition as little more than a brazen defense of capital over the interests of the Bolivian people. This forced capital to change strategy, which it did rather effectively. The Bolivian opposition organized by using the autonomy movement as a new cover for its underlying aims. It then bided its time. By 2019, it found the opportunity Morales provided for them, and it took it. The U.S. left – had it built a solidarity movement with Bolivia – might have fought USAID more effectively in Bolivian than in Venezuela. Why? Venezuela's close connection to the oil economy made it a higher priority of capital and more attractive target for U.S. intervention. Barriers to leftist victory in Bolivia were thus somewhere lower. But the U.S. left lacked clear information about the situation in Bolivia and lacked a broad solidarity movement. It didn't even begin developing a strategy or set of pressure tactics.

Latin America: Global Capital and the Pink Tide

Morales first won election in 2005 not as an anomaly. He won, rather, as one of the later victories in the Pink Tide wave across South America. The Pink Tide began its electoral successes[142] with the victory of Hugo Chávez in Venezuela in 1998, continuing with elected leaders like Luiz Inácio Lula da Silva in Brazil. By now, it has declined due to economic recession in the late 2000s and broader economic and social forces[143]. The decline in oil prices in the 2010s stands out as one such powerful force. The Pink Tide produced and reproduced many of the same issues found in Bolivia. Indeed, it's difficult to discuss Morales and Áñez without mentioning the situation elsewhere in South America, particularly in Venezuela. The issues blew up much sooner in most other places. Bolivia held out largely because its ethnic bonds were stronger than the bonds in other countries. And so, it's hardly surprising that the troubles in 2019 Bolivia happened sooner in places like Brazil, Chile, and Ecuador.

Bolivia and Venezuela developed novel, innovative techniques for fighting global capital. The U.S. left can take this away as a key lesson. Readers looking for more depth on these techniques – particularly some of their shortcomings and their tendencies to continue relying too heavily

---

[142] And, prior to its *electoral* successes, it began with a wave of social movements. See Gonzalez 2018 for the deeper story on social movements. See especially p. 142 for emphasis on Brazil's Landless Workers Movement.

[143] Readers would be well advised to look to Rojas 2018 for a deeper story about why the Pink Tide fell apart. Rojas points out – quite correctly – that broader social forces played a larger role than the decisions of individual leaders.

on foreign direct investment – should consult Henry Veltmeyer and James Petras's 2014 book *The New Extractivism*[144]. One key remaining problem in all the Pink Tide nations, but particularly nations like Argentina, Bolivia, and Brazil, is that their resource extraction programs remain tied to global capital. But even when their leftist governments stood too close to domestic capital, Bolivia and Venezuela provided social democratic advances. By clawing back natural resources from global capital – re-establishing democratic ownership over them – they provided a refreshing break from the neoliberal wave of the last few decades. The U.S. left can and should encourage these moves. It can also build them at home. We have countless opportunities to do something similar in the U.S. Cities can turn to, e.g., municipal electricity and public housing. Venezuela innovated in this space in the early 2000s. From this, the U.S. left can learn how to use power to achieve public ownership.

---

[144] Veltmeyer and Petras 2014.

Chapter 5

Middle East

Many Americans think of the Middle East as the world's major 'hotspot' for war. When U.S. leftists think about the region, thoughts drift to major wars in Afghanistan and Iraq and potential war in Iran. Most of our anti-war mobilization of the last two decades focused on the Middle East. All this makes sense in light of heavy press coverage of conflict and loss of life in the region. The press spends a large amount of time on it, even when deadlier wars take place elsewhere. Why? As we'll see, the Middle East in general – and Israel/Palestine in particular – is central to U.S. interests. As leftists, we need to think broadly about the region's strategic important and the U.S.'s overall approach.

In this chapter, we'll focus on the situation in Israel/Palestine as our central example from the region. From there, we'll move on to Syria. The wars in Afghanistan and Iraq grab our attention, but most leftists – at least in the case of Iraq – already rightly oppose these wars. I'd like to focus instead on cases with more potential for debate and learning. Many leftists are interested in Israel/Palestine, but they lack some of the relevant background. We can help with that here. Israel/Palestine also stands out as the center of power in the region – a major part of why it's so important to U.S. foreign policy. The U.S. uses Israel as its primary tool to achieve its interests in the Middle East. In Syria, the U.S. operates indirectly – in the midst of a Civil War – through various proxies. But no matter how well the U.S. hides its involvement, Israel/Palestine and Syria show the

U.S.'s handiwork. Conflicts in these nations represent deeper, harmful effects of U.S. influence and intervention.

As in Latin America, leftists should use international solidarity and anti-interventionism as key tools when working through Middle East policy. However, we must add pluralism to the top of our list when discussing the Middle East. We need to challenge U.S. hegemony and help build a more pluralistic world. Middle Eastern conflicts operate against a background of U.S. hegemony – a background we looked at in Chapter 2. A regional hegemon – Israel – largely dominates the region. But the U.S. – a *world* hegemon – stands behind Israel, often using it as a proxy to serve its own interests. By examining the situation on the ground, the left can gain insights. A primary insight is that local liberation struggles carry broader implications for larger structures of world power.

Israel/Palestine

For years, U.S. policy on the Israeli-Palestinian conflict served as a shining example of the bipartisan foreign policy consensus. From conservative to progressive, for many years American politicians endorsed the U.S.'s policy of providing aid and diplomatic cover to Israel in exchange for Israel's promotion of U.S. interests in the region. But more recently, the conflict emerged as a major point of contention between liberal and leftist camps. At this end of the political spectrum, the consensus starting breaking up. Liberals still endorse it. Leftists increasingly do not. The U.S. left now largely embraces Palestinian liberation movements.

But I've gotten a bit ahead of myself. Disagreement about the situation in Israel/Palestine runs deeper than one over mere strategic priorities or even political viewpoints. The various sides of the conflict disagree over even the basic facts on the ground. That's much more serious, and it's an issue we need to settle to some degree before we have a fruitful discussion. Writing from conservative, liberal, progressive, and leftist perspectives seems to involve navigating new worlds and distinct sets of self-serving historical facts. To be clear, these issues crop up in many political topics, and we can manage most of them. But it's far worse on this topic than others. As a result, I'll start with modest aims. I'll provide readers with a basic sense of the conflict, with a focus on where the U.S. left might help. The interpretation I'll provide is, of course, a leftist one that's critical of U.S. foreign policy. This means we'll need to take sides in some of the historical disputes, though we should carefully consider the evidence when doing so.

For a basic leftist political orientation on Israel/Palestine, I'll recommend readers consult one key book – Noam Chomsky's 1983 classic, *The Fateful Triangle*[145]. Chomsky orients readers to the conflict, focusing on the 1960s and 1970s. Most of today's events trace back to the 1967 Six-Day war and its aftermath. Chomsky sets the ground both for the major events of the 1980s and the still lingering elements of the conflict. Chomsky's leftist foreign policy credentials are, of course, sterling. He takes strong stances on the issues, though that's hardly a problem for our purposes. The book doesn't apply in its entirety today, due to changes in the relationship between Israel and the U.S. We'll address those issues later. But Chomsky lays out the basic players and the games they still play, providing us with our first important lesson of the Israeli-Palestinian conflict: it has three participants, not two. We call it the 'Israeli-Palestinian conflict,' but it's really a conflict between Israel, the Palestinians, and the U.S. Not merely referee or judge, the U.S. joined as an active participant in the 1960s, and it actively participated to an even larger degree in the 1980s. Until the 1990s, we might argue it was the primary participant. But it remains actively involved today. Far from a solver of problems, the U.S. *creates* problems. It does so from the 'side' of Israel, or at least the side of the Israeli state[146].

Liberals and Leftists on the Israeli-Palestinian Conflict

The Israeli-Palestine conflict opens up new lines of division between leftist and liberal foreign policy approaches. Liberals distinguish between

---

[145] Chomsky 2014 [1983].

[146] As we'll discuss later, the key issue for Chomsky's book is that the conflict has changed form in various ways over the past 20-30 years. The U.S. role – while still large – isn't as large as it was in the 1970s and 1980s. Israel has asserted increasing independence and increasingly carves out its own interests outside those of the U.S. Furthermore, the Soviet Union is obviously no longer a factor in the way it once was.

'good' and 'bad' actors on both the Israeli and Palestinian sides. They place allegedly 'center-left' organizations like the Israeli Labour Party on the 'good' side. At times, they also place 'moderate Palestinians' like Fatah on the good side, though this varies. By contrast, they place far-right organizations on the 'bad' side. This includes the Israeli Likud Party and some of the smaller right-wing religious and nationalist parties. They also place 'hardline' Palestinian groups like Hamas on the bad side. Some – those more openly sympathetic to Israel and derisive toward the Palestinian cause – even put Fatah here. In drawing these distinctions, liberals operate according to a basic model of the conflict. They think the 'good' actors want to achieve piece, but the 'bad' actors stymie the good ones. In this liberal model, the peaceful team wants something much like Bill Clinton's 2000 proposal while the other team profits from conflict and war[147].

The model provides liberals with an operating theory and explanation of the conflict itself. Liberals explain it in terms of things like religious dogma and opposition, poor lines of communication, lack of cultural understanding, and so on. With few exceptions, liberals avoid appealing to identity, economics, or anything resembling, e.g., postcolonial theory. Notably, even though I've called this a 'liberal' approach, it's not specific to liberals. Many U.S. conservatives share these attitudes. It's the approach of the bipartisan foreign policy consensus, an approach many conservatives and liberals alike endorse. We see deviation from the approach among far-right wing nationalists in the U.S. We also see right-wingers who take a more negative attitude toward Fatah. But most U.S. conservatives and liberals adhere closely to this basic model and approach.

The problem – and what makes writing about the conflict so difficult in the U.S. – is that the bipartisan foreign policy consensus is wrong from top to bottom about the Israeli-Palestinian conflict. The Israeli Labour

---

[147] The 2000 Clinton Parameters were supposed to be a framework for negotiations between Israel and Palestine. The Parameters would establish Palestinian rule over most of the West Bank. But they would retain Israeli control over some West Bank settlements and over various 'buffer zones' between the two nations. For an overview, see: https://israelipalestinian.procon.org/background-resources/the-clinton-parameters/. Last accessed July 30, 2020.

Party actively *opposes* peace. It has stood for decades as a leader of the opposition to a peaceful resolution. It led Israel through a 1956 invasion of Egypt, and then the 1967 invasion of Egypt, Jordan, and Syria. After seizing Palestinian territories in the Gaza Strip and West Bank in 1967, Israel built a series of illegal settlements under Labour Party governance[148]. To this day, these settlements – which Israeli governments across the political spectrum expanded – remain a key point a contention. In the 50+ years since these major wars, Labour remained a hawkish party. Its leader in a string of elections in 2019-2020 confirmed this history, presenting no meaningful alternative to the status quo[149]. In light of these facts, how Labour qualifies as a 'good' actor on any serious theory remains a head-scratcher.

And yet, Israel's far-right pushes even *further* to the right than Labour. Likud and its allies invite comparisons to the some of the world's worst regimes. Benjamin Netanyahu, for instance, repeatedly threatens to annex the West Bank and expel its population with military force. These threats – if carried out – would result in violent conflict and death to the point of genocide. And while it's convenient for many people to blame Netanyahu the individual, he represents Israel's right-wing as a whole on this issue. It has long held as a goal the annexation of the West Bank and removal of its Palestinian population. Only during a brief period in the early 2000s did the Israeli right arrive at a slightly less terrible policy[150]. Otherwise, Netanyahu's stance remains in line with the historical Israeli right in the 1970s and 1980s. U.S. liberals condemn this, and they do so correctly. But they miss the fact that this differs from Labour's policy in degree rather than kind. Internal disagreement in mainstream Israeli politics generally concerns whether to displace and remove Palestinians at once or gradually through illegal settlement, not whether to do it at all.

---

[148] For an overview of how Israeli settlements violate international law, see: https://www.amnesty.org/en/latest/campaigns/2019/01/chapter-3-israeli-settlements-and-international-law/. Last accessed: July 30, 2020.

[149] The leader, Amir Peretz, was once seen as a promotor of peace. However, a stint as Defense Minister pushed him into the hawk camp.

[150] Specifically, Ariel Sharon led right-wing forces in Israel toward disengagement from the Gaza Strip as a new policy.

The various players came together in the 1990s and early 2000s to negotiate a wide range of peace deals and policy reforms. Many Americans know, for example, the Oslo Accords and Clinton Parameters. These efforts, however, remained in line with the bipartisan foreign policy consensus in the U.S. They didn't depart significantly from the standard line. One might consult, for example, Edward Said's work on Oslo for a greater sense of how this worked. Said documented how Israeli and U.S. interests drove the 'peace process.' And he documented the overall attitude toward Palestinians – that they are, at best, unwelcome guests in their own lands[151]. U.S. liberals focused excessively on things like decorum or religion managed to completely miss most of these background facts and conditions.

So, what are the alternatives to the bipartisan foreign policy consensus? I've mentioned far-right nationalism, which obviously isn't the direction in which the U.S. left wants to head. Leftist alternatives remain divided and fragmented, but I think we can pick out two kinds of approaches. The first is a racial and/or colonial frame. We might, for example, draw analogies between Israeli treatment of Palestinians and U.S. treatment of non-whites. However, in doing this we risk imposing an American racial framework on an area of the world where it doesn't quite fit. More commonly, people draw analogies between the situation in the Palestinian territories and the one in Apartheid South Africa. Jimmy Carter himself took up this line of thought in recent years[152], and we also saw this approach in the 2016 platform of the Movement for Black Lives[153]. The analogy works more effectively than the one on U.S. racism, but it doesn't account for the full range of issues. The Gaza Strip *does* resemble a South African Bantustan[154] in many respects. In particular, Palestinian 'self-rule' co-exists with Israeli domination in a way quite similar to the Bantustans.

---

[151] In particular, see Said 1996.

[152] See Carter 2006.

[153] https://web.archive.org/web/20160828130300/https://policy.m4bl.org/invest-divest/. Last accessed: July 30, 2020. The Movement for Black Lives appears to have removed this material from its 2020 platform.

[154] The Apartheid government of South Africa established Bantustans as segregated communities for various ethnic groups. See: https://www.sahistory.org.za/article/homelands. Last accessed: July 30, 2020. See also Ally and Lissoni 2017.

But the West Bank hardly resembles a Bantustan at all. In some respects, its situation is worse. Palestinians hold less self-rule in the West Bank than black South Africans did in most Bantustans.

Alternatively – or in addition to racial frames – we might frame Israeli treatment of Palestinians in settler-colonial terms. Readers might recall our discussion of settler-colonialism in Bolivia in Chapter 4. In a settler-colonial framework, an outside dominant power clears the land of its native population and resettles that land with its own people[155]. The framework applies rather well to this region. Much of the Israeli right – and even some of its center – wants to clear the land of its native Palestinian population and replace that population with Israeli citizens. It wants to replace the population with mostly Jewish Israeli citizens, or so the frame says. And in fact, Israel has taken on many traits of a settler-colonialist state. We see this in its domination of Palestinian political and social life, which it accompanies with racist attitudes. The reality of Israeli settlements – along with Israeli far-right intentions to literally clear the land – thereby suggests Israel has indeed taken on a settler-colonialist project[156]. And so, I think this frame is more useful for us than a direct analogy between U.S. and Israeli racism.

However, we need to qualify the settler-colonialist reading in several ways. First, Israeli politics remain unsettled over whether – and to what degree – to explicitly commit to a settler-colonialist project. The Israeli far-right favors it. But the Israeli center and center-left want something less obviously brutal. And Israel's U.S. allies lean closer to the Israeli center and center-left than they do to the far-right. Donald Trump and far-right nationalists make for a possible exception to this rule. But it's an exception rather than the norm. A Democratic president would likely reset

---

[155] For a more thorough overview of settler-colonialism as applied to Israel/Palestine, I'd recommend the essays in Awad and bean 2020. In particular, these essays explain the origins of Israel prior to World War II in settler-colonial terms (p. 16), present the tenets of Zionism as essentially settler-colonial (p. 22-24), and provide a more thorough model of the types or degrees of settler-colonialism.

[156] Israel also opened the door for a more formal settler-colonial project in its dealings with President Trump in 2020, where Trump appeared to green-light formal annexation of the West Bank.

U.S. policy to the prior norm, and Joe Biden will likely confirm this[157]. Second, the U.S. still plays a large role in the conflict. From the early 1970s through the late 1990s, Israel arguably didn't even have a policy toward the Palestinians independent from U.S. guidance. Its policy existed mostly as an extension of U.S. interests in the region. The U.S. sponsored Israel, giving it billions in aid to carry out U.S. aims. Israel now exerts much more independence from U.S. influence, but the U.S. still gives billions in aid and still acts as Israel's primary *diplomatic* sponsor[158]. The U.S. swats down and vetoes U.N. Security Council resolutions aimed at peace and pushing Israel to follow international law[159]. And so, even if Israel carries out a settler-colonialist project in the region, we might ask whether it's an *Israeli* project at all. Perhaps we would argue that it's really a U.S. project where Israel primarily holds the role of a means to American ends. Third, we simply must consider the complex issues around the founding of Israel. Israel was founded in 1948, and many of its residents were Holocaust survivors. Founders carved the nation from the U.K.'s Palestine Mandate under rather obviously non-ideal conditions. And so, Israel's population comprised mostly marginalized people. In this case, literally a group of people Nazi Germany attempted to exterminate. It's well beyond the scope of the present project, but we should at least consider the question of whether – and to what extent – a severely oppressed population can itself compose a large part of a colonial force.

Economic Approach to the Israeli-Palestinian Conflict

For a second leftist approach, many leftists employ an economic frame. This approach might stand on its own, or we might combine it with a limited appeal to settler-colonialism. In theory, one might also combine it with an analogy to U.S. racism, but that combination is rather strained.

---

[157] As of March 2021, Biden hasn't yet moved the U.S. Embassy in Israel back from Jerusalem to Tel Aviv. And so, if anything, Biden has landed somewhere between resetting U.S. policy to the prior norm and embracing Trump's attitude toward Israel.

[158] On U.S. funding of Israel, see: https://www.everycrsreport.com/reports/RL33222.html. Last accessed: July 30, 2020.

[159] For a list of all UN Security Council resolutions concerning Israel, see: https://en.wikipedia.org/wiki/List_of_United_Nations_resolutions_concerning_Israel. Last accessed: July 30, 2020.

The economic approach reads the conflict as one over *resources*. Israeli and U.S. interests mediate this conflict over resources as the relevant hegemons. Farmland and water comprise the relevant resources in the region, with the West Bank rich in farmland and the Jordan River forming the region's border. Israel depended heavily on these resources during the first three decades of its economic development, but it shrouded its resource policies in the language of defense and security. Far from being about security, in truth this involved securing and defending good farmland and access to the Jordan River. Israel developed the means to acquire and protect these resources. Due to these background conditions, I'll argue in this section that the economic approach is promising and largely correct.

If this seems like an abstract point, we can consult accurate maps of the West Bank, which readers can do at the link in the footnote[160]. The maps show that Israel arranged its settlements in a distinct pattern. Settlements encircle choice farmland near the border, and Israel staggers them along the Jordan River. This serves the purpose of monopolizing farmland and water. By contrast, Israel isolates the Palestinian areas. One might argue this serves security functions. But Israel does not isolate the Palestinians from Israel itself. Rather, it blocks them from the resources they need to replicate Israel's rapid economic development. Nevertheless, we must keep in mind the historical, legacy nature of the settlements. Israel put them in place during a time when those resources were more important than they are now. Since that time, Israel developed a modern tech economy. Indeed, the Israeli economy turned into one of the most advanced, modern tech economies in the world. And so, it no longer depends on these resources to the extent it once did. Despite these contemporary changes, economic development still plays a key role in a good analysis. As it lessened its dependence on farmland and water, Israel strategically ceded certain areas to limited Palestinian autonomy. It accepted more shared rule. This is why Israel turned the Gaza Strip into something like a Bantustan. It's also why Israel turned over parts of the West Bank to partial Palestinian self-rule.

---

[160] https://www.cjpme.org/mapss. Last accessed: December 2, 2020.

Israel's relationship with the Palestinians thereby changed in the last couple of decades. But Israel never totally cut off its dependence on resources and on the Palestinian people themselves. Israeli firms still depend on Palestinian labor, especially in the manual and service sectors[161]. And so, the economic frame offers the left another helpful point of reference. This explains much of the internal debate within Israeli politics. Until it totally cuts itself off from these dependencies, the Israeli far-right's goals remain impractical. They cannot yet convince the Israeli system of the need to annex and clear the land. Israeli capital simply won't stand for it. We see, then, similarities between Israeli capital and U.S. capital with respect to immigrant labor, issues we examined in Chapter 3. Israeli capital wants a certain level of *flow* without *rights*. The operations of regional and global capital proceed underneath the appearance of defense and security. After some digging, we can uncover these operations.

The economic framework provides us with bonuses as well. It offers us tools to explain Israeli control over the Golan Heights, a piece of land that – on the map – looks small and unimportant. The Golan Heights sits between Israel, Jordan, Lebanon, and Syria. It carries a small population. But, despite all this, competing powers long fought over it. We might infer, then, that it holds strategic importance. It certainly once held such importance for Israel, which has occupied the Golan Heights since 1967, justifying its occupation in the usual terms of defense and security. As its name suggests, the Golan Heights towers over the region as a highland, overlooking key strategic points in all the border nations.

This reasoning made sense in 1967, but it makes far less sense today. 50-60 years ago, each nation wanted to hold the high ground. High ground immensely boosted their abilities of communication and surveillance. But with a modern tech economy, high ground is less important than it once was. Israel holds the resources it needs to run an effective surveillance

---

161   https://www.thenewhumanitarian.org/investigations/2017/08/02/occupied-labour-treadmill-palestinian-work-israel; https://www.hrw.org/report/2015/04/13/ripe-abuse/palestinian-child-labor-israeli-agricultural-settlements-west-bank; https://www.jacobinmag.com/2020/05/israel-palestinian-workers-pandemic. All last accessed: July 30, 2020.

program without holding the Golan Heights. All this raises a few questions for us. Why doesn't Israel yield the Heights? One might think Israel needs to build goodwill and rapport with its neighbors. Why not do so by yielding ground no longer critical to its security needs? Yielding the Golan Heights might advance peace and build better relations between Israel and the international community. Aside from the U.S. – nearly always an intransigent outlier, as we've seen – the international community considers the Golan Heights part of Syria. They declare it under Israeli occupation.

With the economic frame in hand, we can see Israel retains the Golan Heights in order to access resources. The Heights are rich in oil and water. Israel began settlement activity in the 1970s. At the time, these settlements were limited, and Israel based them on strategic considerations. However, Israel ramped up activity after 2016. It went so far as to try naming a settlement after Donald Trump in order to stroke Trump's ego and curry U.S. favor[162]. Why? Israel discovered major oil reserves in the Golan Heights in 2016. The interests of capital don't stray far from the surface. Israel's need for the Golan Heights shifted quickly.

Finally, we might combine the economic frame with a settler-colonial one. The economic frame explains very well much of what's happening in the West Bank. And it does so without need to appeal to any additional frame. But a broader settler-colonial frame provides useful answers for some of the divergences between the Gaza Strip and the West Bank. The U.S. left should use both of these frames as key resources. Bringing these things together – the underlying operations of capital, a settler-colonial regime, and the managing of international attitudes – allows us to multiply our understanding in useful ways. We can use this to make sense of a complicated and dense region. And then we can form new relationships and take action on the basis of our grasp of the situation.

---

[162] https://theintercept.com/2019/04/23/netanyahu-trump-golan-heights-illegal-settlement/. Last accessed: October 26, 2020.

Israel/Palestine and the Benefits of Anti-Interventionism and Pluralism

As leftists, we shouldn't forget the importance of international solidarity with Palestinian liberation movements. And we largely *haven't* forgotten. U.S. leftists have many chances to get involved with Palestinian solidarity. Many already know about these chances and do get involved. Many leftists know the Boycott, Divestment, and Sanctions (BDS) movement[163], a Palestinian-led campaign using international law and solidarity with other anti-oppression movements as tools for action. The DSA in the U.S. endorsed BDS at its 2017 National Convention[164], drawing larger attention to BDS among the socialist left. BDS thus serves as a useful starting point for many on the U.S. left. Beyond the DSA, however, U.S. racial justice movements stand at the forefront of solidarity with Palestine. I mentioned earlier the 2016 statement from the Movement for Black Lives. In fact, racial justice movements – from the civil rights era to the Black Lives Matter era – have increasingly built bonds of solidarity and action with the Palestinian liberation movement[165].

We should also appeal to our principles of anti-interventionism and pluralism. They serve as our most useful principles on issues related to Israel and Palestine. *The Fateful Triangle*[166] cleared up a key point of deception from the U.S. press and U.S. politics. The U.S. presents itself as a bold defender of the 'peace process,' actively working to resolve the Israeli-Palestinian conflict. The Clinton Administration took up this deception very effectively when conducting the Oslo Accords and later laying out an ambitious roadmap via the Clinton Parameters. Overall, the U.S. presents its intentions as good and its 'solutions' as beneficial. Nothing could be further from the truth. The U.S. long promoted Israel

---

[163] https://bdsmovement.net/. Last accessed: June 6, 2020.

[164] https://bdsmovement.net/news/democratic-socialists-america-commit-national-bds-organizing. Last accessed: June 6, 2020

[165] For a broad history of Black-Palestinian solidarity, see Fischbach 2018. For an overview of the Freedom is our Future platform of the US Campaign for Palestinian rights, see Awad and bean 2020, pp. 192-193. And for an essay collection situating Palestinian solidarity within anti-racist and prison abolitionist movements, see Davis 2016. See also: https://www.arabnews.com/node/1690701. Last accessed: July 30, 2020.

[166] Chomsky 2014 [1983].

as a regional hegemon. It provided funding and diplomatic cover for Israel, and it used Israel as a sharp tool to promote its own policy aims. It did so largely undetected, without serious, critical discussion at the national level. This remains a testament to the need for the U.S. left to advocate for a non-interventionist foreign policy[167]. The case shows the U.S. can pass off almost *anything* as a positive, humanitarian intervention. And so, leftists must give close, critical scrutiny to *any* kind of intervention.

Multiple pieces of the Israeli-Palestinian conflict demonstrate the need for a greater balance of power among nations. These highlight the importance of pluralism to a U.S. left foreign policy. An imbalance of power between Israel and the U.S. enabled the U.S. to use Israel as a tool for much of its history. From the 1970s, the U.S. did often advance the interests of the Israeli state, but it did so only after achieving its own interests. Indeed, many of the policies the U.S. supported endangered Israel in both the short- and long-term. The U.S. also made other moves in the region – such as pouring funding and diplomatic support into Egypt after 1979[168] – that the Israeli state may not itself have endorsed. Israel made gains from U.S. sponsorship, but it also ceded control. Fighting for the return of this control became a key goal of its internal development. The Israeli economy made major gains in the last few decades, narrowing the power gap between Israel and the U.S. To some degree, it now pursues policies not directed by the U.S. When it elects leaders like Benjamin Netanyahu, this presents new dangers. Indeed, Israel's rise as a more autonomous regional hegemon has not benefited the world overall. But it did free up Israel to make (often very small) moves in the right direction. Moving to limited Palestinian self-governance in the Gaza Strip offered a few small advances. Of course, Israeli domination of borders largely negated any positive impact.

We need greater pluralism even more desperately as it concerns relations between Israel and Palestine. Israel always held an advantage over the Palestinians. In fact, Egypt, Jordan, Israel, and the Palestinians

---

[167] A non-interventionist foreign policy also helps Palestinians overcome some of their internal divisions, a move that can strengthen campaigns like BDS. See Awad and bean 2020, p. 116.

[168] For an overview of U.S. funding of Egypt, see: https://www.state.gov/u-s-relations-with-egypt/. Last accessed: July 30, 2020.

were never on an equal footing. Israel long enjoyed advantages in military might, power, and territory. But prior to the 1967 and 1973 wars, these advantages were much smaller than they are today. Despite more volatile relations, they achieved something closer to parity. Israel and Egypt attempted multiple times to conquer one another, and they failed. We don't want to fully return to this situation, but we can learn from it. We can see the benefits of greater balance. Increasing the power of Palestine relative to Israel would help Palestine gain recognition and support from international institutions. It would thereby increase its chances at real liberation from foreign occupation.

If the U.S. left makes one key demand of U.S. policy in Israel/Palestine, it should demand the U.S. quit blocking peace. This stands out as the central policy goal of the U.S. left in the region. Leftists can join international solidarity movements with Palestinians, especially those led by racial justice groups. They can join movements like BDS and build those movements into a regular part of U.S. leftist groups. Groups like the DSA increasingly incorporate solidarity into their everyday work, and this integration should continue. The DSA, in particular, holds a place of key importance in the socialist left in the U.S. Through the DSA, the U.S. left can press for a more active role for official U.S. policy, but this presents us with dangers. Too many people still think the U.S. *already* plays a positive role in the world. Even many leftists still believe this. And so, the dangerously low level of political education in the U.S. stands out as a major barrier. This leaves us with firm anti-interventionism as our best short-term tool. We need to focus on preventing the U.S. from doing harm in the world until we can build a positive alternative.

A Note on Proportionality

Many people criticize Palestinian solidarity movements on grounds of 'proportionality.' They claim critics of Israel focus too heavily on Israeli oppression of Palestinians, claiming they do so to the exclusion of other wrongs in the world. These criticisms mostly come from the political right, but they sometimes come from the left. Michael Walzer is a widely-respected figure on the political left who utilizes this criticism. We examined his work briefly in Chapter 2, where we saw that a principle of symmetry animates his work. And he applies that principle to issues involving Israel and Palestine. He argues leftists focus on Israeli wrongs to the exclusion of wrongs from, e.g., Syria or Russia. He – along with other critics – suggests that leftists who do this display anti-Semitism, whether explicitly or implicitly.

With the tools of this chapter handy, I think we can see the problem with the analysis of Walzer and other critics. The Middle East is *strategically* important, and usually more so than other regions. From a U.S. foreign policy perspective, it stands out as the most important region because it is a major site of conflict over resources. And Israel remains the U.S.'s most important ally in the region. The U.S. long operated through Israel to achieve its own interests, and Israel became the regional hegemon. Thus, we'd expect leftists to spend a great deal of time discussing U.S.-Israel issues, especially Israeli harms to Palestinians. It would be a greater mystery if Israel *weren't* central to U.S. left foreign policy discussions.

However, I do think the U.S. left – and Israel critics – often make one key mistake. And perhaps we can learn this as a lesson from Walzer's criticism. The U.S. left tends to overestimate Israeli influence on the U.S. Many leftists – and other critics of Israel[169] – extensively discuss an 'Israel lobby.' They sometimes charge the Israel lobby with directing U.S. policy in the region. This often reverses the causal order of events in the world. To speak of an Israel lobby as a major player in the conflict is to set aside the fact that the U.S. itself sets the tone. Of course, many lobbyists in Washington D.C. work on behalf of Israeli interests. But they do so because the U.S. remains the key *site of power*. Every supplicant goes to the U.S. with their petition. Lobbying achieves results, but it doesn't ultimately direct power. If the U.S. left overestimates the importance of pro-Israel lobbyists, it will apply pressure at the wrong points. The left must properly analyze power to achieve results.

---

[169] See, for example, Mearsheimer and Walt 2008.

Syria and Civil War

The possibility of war lurks in the background of foreign policy discussion involving Syria, more than any nation other than perhaps Iran. The situation began in 2011 with the Syrian civil war, and it has persisted in the decade since then. We'll examine this situation in depth and discover a more complicated truth. In fact, less than a looming *possibility*, war has been more a hardly noticed *reality*. We'll find that the situation in Syria reveals both the durability of the bipartisan foreign policy consensus and a series of fissures in it. Those fissures began during the Obama presidency, and they continued in varying forms under Trump and Biden. We'll look at these developments and draw several lessons.

The situation in Syria dates to the middle of the 20th century, to a long period of single-party rule[170]. The Arab Socialist Ba'ath Party ruled Syria in some form since a 1963 coup. Events disrupted that rule on several occasions, but they never broke it. The Ba'ath Party never displayed the dynastic and nepotistic leanings of, for example, the ruling party in North Korea. Despite that, the al-Assad family took over rule a half century ago and never yielded power. Hafez al-Assad ruled for about 30 years, and his son Bashar has now ruled for about 20. In addition, the Ba'ath Party retains 'socialist' in its title, but one thing we can say about the party is that it's *not socialist*. A few socialists do endorse Bashar al-Assad. But they don't endorse him due to any socialist policies. Rather, they endorse him due to opposition to him from U.S. foreign policy experts. The Ba'ath Party uses the word 'socialist' for historical reasons analogous to why various Western parties still carry the title 'social democratic' despite not advocating social democracy. When Ba'athists seized Syria in the late 1960s and 1970s, the party had socialist factions. Some of its key leaders carried strong ties to pan-Arab socialist groups and broader leftist movements[171]. As they assumed and consolidated rule, the al-Assad family cut those ties. Instead, they focused on the consolidation of class interests

---

[170] For a compact history of 20th century Syrian politics, readers are well advised to consult Gopal 2020, especially pp. 112-118.
[171] Mansur al-Atrash and Salah Jadid stand out in particular as leftist leaders within the context of the Syrian Ba'ath movement.

around the regime[172]. By the early 2000s, they had removed almost all aspects of Syrian socialism.

When Syria transitioned power from Hafez to his son Bashar, some Syrian dissidents and international observers raised their hopes. They thought Bashar al-Assad might accept democratic reforms and more humane policies. Even al-Assad himself sent messages and signals in this direction. But events on the ground crushed this optimism in quick order. In office, al-Assad took all the moves we might expect from a dynastic ethno-state. Some of his moves included: consolidating authority and power around the dominant group, appointing cronies and family friends to important positions, putting allies in party offices, et al. The civil war then ended any faint glimmer of hope that remained. The U.S. left should think about the Syrian Civil War in the context of the broader Arab Spring movement. The Tunisian Revolution kicked it off in 2010-2011, with the Spring then fanning through the Middle East and North Africa. It represented both the fruit of years of organizing and a quick outburst. We should take away from this the lesson that prior bonds of international solidarity remain key. It's not enough to wait for a trigger event. We must put the organizing pieces in place first[173].

Al-Assad policy in the neoliberal era played a major role in setting the conditions that led to a Syrian uprising. Hafez al-Assad stripped the party and country of its leftist intellectual and policy base[174]. These changes paved the way for a sharp spike in inequality, and inequality stood out as the major force driving most of the Arab Spring uprisings. Specifically, al-Assad financialized and privatized the Syrian economy. This produced a sharp split between a Damascus-based ownership class and a dispossessed class in the rest of the country. The split led to resentment and exploitation, and Syrians could see how geography marked these features.

---

[172] See Gopal 2020, pp. 115-116.

[173] Readers would be well advised to consult feminist sources related to the Arab Spring. For an introduction to these perspectives, see: Maravankin 2017 and https://lb.boell.org/en/2017/01/18/between-trauma-and-resistance-feminist-engagement-arab-spring. Last accessed: July 30, 2020.

[174] Particularly critical to these changes were the encouragement of foreign direct investment and the taking of land from poorer Syrians. See Gopal 2020, pp. 118-120.

Syria added a second site of inequality to this already dangerous situation – a divide between an Alawite minority ruling class and a dispossessed majority. Non-Alawaite Syrians hold almost no positions of power or influence in the nation. Furthermore, the Syrian 'majority' itself divides into many smaller groups. Like most Americans, the U.S. left thinks about the Middle East in terms of two or three major branches of Islam. But the situation in Syria – as well as Lebanon, which raises different issues – is much more complex. Syria contains many Muslim and non-Muslim groups, and this creates administrative challenges. Bashar al-Assad never effectively resolved the tensions this broad situation created.

The Syrian Civil War began as a series of political protests grounded in these divisions and inequalities[175]. But the protests didn't produce a civil war on their own[176]. Pre-emptive overreaction by the al-Assad regime stepped in as a major cause. Al-Assad saw the looming danger. In response, he arrested and tortured political dissidents, students, and other groups. He did so to prevent a Syrian branch of the Arab Spring. And he obviously failed. These moves backfired, and al-Assad introduced a series of concessions and reforms. By this point, however, no one bought it. In response, forces internal to the al-Assad regime defected and created a Free Syrian Army. At first, the defectors wanted to keep most of the regime in place, but replace al-Assad as its leader. Full warfare and international intervention followed. Syria spiraled out of control, creating the conditions for ISIS and U.S. involvement by 2014. Eventually, al-Assad emerged victorious, or close enough to victorious to reclaim control of much of the country. But the war took a catastrophic toll, leaving high death and displacement numbers and an active ISIS and Turkish military presence in the country.

---

[175] For an overview of the Syrian Civil War centered on the perspectives of ordinary Syrians, see Pearlman 2017. On her website, Pearlman also includes helpful teaching and reading guides for the book. See: https://sites.northwestern.edu/wendypearlman/. Last accessed July 30, 2020.

[176] There's a separate question of *why* the protests weren't sufficient to produce a civil war or overturn the regime. Gopal 2020 argues convincingly that the elements that composed the Syrian opposition – non-Damascus bourgeoisie and precarious workers – didn't have sufficient leverage to topple the regime. See Gopal 2020, pp. 124-129.

U.S. Foreign and Military Aid to Syria

The U.S. public lacks a solid grasp of the U.S.'s role in Syria. Many Americans – even leftists – believe the U.S. remains mostly passive. They think the U.S. supports 'moderate Syrians' or the 'Syrian opposition,' avoiding direct conflict or high levels of military aid. When the press discusses these issues, it does so on the tacit assumption that war remains a future possibility for the U.S. rather than a current reality. The assumption held most notably during discussion of Obama's actual and potential interventions in the civil war. Unfortunately, these tacit assumptions are largely false. In fact, the U.S. began intervening from nearly the beginning of the conflict[177]. And U.S. intervention escalated quickly. It all started seemingly innocent enough, with U.S. food aid to the Free Syrian Army beginning almost as soon as the group formed in 2011. There was a large time gap between these initial moves and formal military assistance and training programs in 2014. But readers should recall our discussion of Jessica Trisko Darden's book from Chapter 2. Darden argued persuasively that the kind of economic and logistical assistance the U.S. provides often leads to more deaths. It does so via a variety of routes, notably the redirection of aid to military purposes. Far from a looming possibility, then, the U.S. began active participation in Syrian death and destruction about a decade ago.

U.S. action in Syria shows a recurrence of the old patterns and mistakes of U.S. interventionism. These mistakes happen so often we can build a narrative around them. How does this narrative go? The U.S. encourages – or even outright fabricates – 'moderates' sympathetic to U.S. interests in the region. It then heavily funds these groups. However, opponents expose the groups as having little or no grassroots support among the local population. The groups fold, or 'rebel' enemies less sympathetic to U.S. interests defeat them. And we find this narrative playing out for

---

[177] This is another area where Wikipedia stands out as a surprisingly helpful source. See: https://en.wikipedia.org/wiki/American-led_intervention_in_the_Syrian_Civil_War; https://en.wikipedia.org/wiki/Timeline_of_the_American-led_intervention_in_the_Syrian_Civil_War. Both last accessed: July 30, 2020.

decades. Vietnam remains the most obvious and tragic instance[178]. In Vietnam, U.S. intervention cost hundreds of thousands – probably millions – of lives. People paid the cost when the Deng government needed massive U.S. financial and military assistance to survive.

How did it happen in Syria? The U.S. funded and supported the group we call the 'Free Syrian Army.' At least, this was accurate enough in the beginning. A group of military officers created the Free Syrian Army to overthrow al-Assad and maintain Syria's underlying social structure. It wanted a version of the status quo a bit more responsive to popular demand. The U.S. might not *love* this state of affairs, but it could effectively turn it into something useful for its interests. But all this quickly became more fantasy than reality. The Free Syrian Army now exists mostly on paper. The original group fell apart months after defectors created it, and a wide variety of groups now use the 'Free Syrian Army' label. These groups hold any number of attitudes toward governance, war, and U.S. interests in the region. They have little grassroots support, and they depend entirely on U.S. funding to continue operations. Indeed, all these groups hold little in common other than commitment to receiving U.S. aid.

But even this understates the actual level and scope of U.S. intervention in Syria. The U.S. does not merely provide economic and logical assistance to groups it calls 'moderate.' It also engages in active military intervention in Syria. Obama began this program in 2014 under the heading of fighting ISIS. ISIS established itself in Syria in the context of a power vacuum, providing the U.S. with all the cover it needed to fight a war *within* Syria without fighting one *against* Syria. It could undermine al-Assad without doing it so obviously as to provoke widespread international condemnation. In the first months of U.S. military intervention – through January 2015 – it carried out 70 airstrikes in Syria. Under the broader program Operation Inherent Resolve, the U.S. carried out a total of 35,000

---

[178] Readers interested in how this played on in Vietnam are well advised to consult Noam Chomsky's work on the topic. See, for example, this interview: https://chomsky.info/198210__/. Last accessed: July 30, 2020.

airstrikes in Iraq and Syria. It turned into a regional operation key to U.S. foreign policy in the Middle East[179].

These events carry two key implications for foreign policy debate in the U.S. These hold for both mainstream politics and leftist politics. First, 'will the U.S. go to war in Syria, and how do we prevent it?' is the wrong question. It's far too late for a question like this one. The U.S. began Syrian operations a decade ago and entered a full-scale war more than 6 years ago. Obama entered the U.S. into this war. Trump – with varying levels of complication, and we'll see below – kept the U.S. in the war. Second, the bipartisan foreign policy consensus mostly held in Syria. It did run into various issues, as we'll see later. Certain voices in U.S. foreign policy – particularly Hillary Clinton, Lindsay Graham, John McCain, and the other usual suspects – called for even harsher intervention that would lead to hundreds of thousands of additional deaths. They likely would have supported even a formal U.S. occupation of the country. Obama and Trump dodged all this, but Obama and Trump policy still advanced the shrewd pursuit of U.S. interests via economic and military intervention. Some praised Obama for his alleged 'restraint' for resisting the push of Clinton and others. And some even criticized Obama for failing to enforce a 'red line[180].' But these differences remain one of degree rather than kind. Obama and Trump carried out policies well within the U.S. mainstream.

The YPG, Restraint, and Withdrawal

And so, much of the U.S. policy situation in Syria remains business as usual. But we can find at least one potential exception. It's an exception the U.S. left should study, learn from, and debate. While failing to create 'moderates,' the U.S. eventually provided funding and support to the Syrian Democratic Forces (SDF). The SDF emerged as the most effective fighting force in the region open to alignment with U.S. interests. It also

---

[179] The U.S. government offers its own overview of the Operation: https://www.inherentresolve.mil/. Last accessed: July 30, 2020.

[180] In the 'red line' controversy, Obama announced that use of chemical weapons by al-Assad would warrant the use of U.S. military forces in Syria. But after such evidence materialized, Obama did not launch a full-scale, Iraq-sized invasion of the nation. Extreme foreign policy hawks criticized Obama for this.

strongly dislikes ISIS, setting it up as a potential coalition partner with the U.S. The enemy of U.S.'s enemies thus became the friend of the U.S. even in the face of potential friction. And indeed, we do find potential friction between the SDF and the U.S.

The Kurdish People's Protection Units (YPG) lead the SDF's military component. The YPG established itself as a broad, anti-fascist coalition. It's composed mostly of ethnic Kurds opposed to al-Assad. However, it opposes ISIS even more strongly than al-Assad, setting itself up as a primarily anti-ISIS group. The YPG focuses almost all its military operations against ISIS, again setting up the potential U.S.-YPG coalition. However, the YPG incorporates leftist elements, garnering curiosity from the U.S. left and suspicion from the U.S. state. It incorporates these elements in various ways, but most prominently through its Women's Protection Units (YPJ).

The YPJ is an explicitly feminist group of women fighters within the broader YPG. The YPJ maintains a complex feminist ideology, which we won't discuss in detail here. But it maintains links to both libertarian socialist groups and to the Kurdistan Workers Party (PKK). It operates with a complex analysis of social scientific work, reading social science as a form of gender-based oppression. This all goes under the headline of 'Jineology[181].' This piece brings these groups together and forms a bridge between the YPJ, PKK, feminism, and military defense. To complicate these matters further, the YPJ isn't the only leftist element within the YPG. The YPG also maintains an international group incorporating leftist elements. Suffice it to say, the YPG is a broad coalition with many moving parts, including some leftist parts.

Thus, a complex web brings together many elements we don't normally see in the same place. For the U.S. left, I think we find potential rewards and risks. We want to encourage the building of power by leftist groups, and we should form bonds with these leftist groups where possible. However, the U.S. will quickly discard the democratic and popular

---

[181] I've written in the past on similar topics. See Drabek 2014. The broad point of such work is to point out that politics infuses social scientific work, particularly the way social scientists classify the people and social groups they study.

elements of the YPG if it gets the opportunity. It promotes these groups only for practical reasons, mostly their ability to wage war against ISIS. We should thus hold an attitude of cautious optimism toward these developments. At the same time, we should remember our basic principles of anti-interventionism and pluralism. Given a strong hand to act, the U.S. will undermine the YPG and the YPJ without hesitation. As a result, it would be better for the U.S. left to build organic links with the YPG and the YPJ than to encourage U.S. funding. It's all the more dangerous to advocate official bonds between the U.S. state and these groups. Without organic links and a leftist narrative in place, many Americans misinterpret minor departures from mainstream foreign policy as major successes. And this happens across the political spectrum. U.S. political discourse presented Obama as a cautious, peace-seeking leader in Syria. And most people in the liberal and progressive camps bought it. Trump manipulated these trends to his own ends. He announced a withdrawal of U.S. troops in Syria in December 2018. He even partially carried it out in October 2019. Trump took a lighter hand in Syria than Obama, but Trump's 'anti-war' streak didn't fully hold up under pressure.

While their motives vary, the underlying direction and point remain consistent. When U.S. politicians operate from a slightly scaled-down realism, they look downright peaceful in comparison to politicians like Hillary Clinton, Lindsay Graham, and John McCain. Overall, U.S. foreign policy remains belligerent. There's a risk the public will read even steps as paltry as those taken by Obama and Trump as a move to the left on foreign policy. Thus, the U.S. left must distinguish its own foreign policy vision from those of Obama and Trump (and Biden). Neither Obama nor Trump grounded their 'less aggressive' foreign policy in anything like international solidarity. They do not practice anti-interventionism, nor do they struggle to build a more pluralistic world. They'll set aside anti-war policy as soon as the situation changes or that policy becomes politically inconvenient for them. Leftists can endorse the restraint shown by U.S. leaders in particular situations. That's fine. But the left needs a deeper story to emphasize its ultimate aims and strategies for reaching those aims.

Middle East: To Peace Via Pluralism

When we look at the Middle East, we find a 'hotspot' of war. The failure to create a pluralistic world plays no small role in that hotspot. The region moved from the colonial, imperial playground of the U.K. and U.S. empires to a series of regional hegemons. The hegemons took over where the empires left off. That legacy looms large over everything that happens in the region. For the U.S. left, our roadmap to peace starts with promoting anti-interventionism. We must pressure the U.S. to stop blocking peace. The U.S. isn't an actor with good intentions. Rather, it promotes policies that serve its own interests regardless of the broader impact. It once used Israel as its major political player, and now Israel serves as the regional hegemon. The U.S. – and, to some extent, now Israel – dominates through wars, military intervention, and systems of economic and humanitarian aid. The U.S. left must pressure the U.S. to exit this system via anti-interventionism. At the same time, the U.S. left can help create a more pluralistic world. It can nurture joint efforts with Palestinian liberation movements, promising Syrian groups, and the movements of other oppressed groups.

Chapter 6

East Asia

We saw in the previous chapters on Latin America and the Middle East a broad overview of how the U.S. implements its foreign policy. The U.S. translates its perceived national interest into an interventionist strategy toward other nations. It uses democratic and humanitarian rhetoric to bolster policies not especially in line with democratic or humanitarian goals. The U.S. left – as a part of its project – needs to reveal these abuses. It can do so along the way to building solidarity with people in the nations in which the U.S. intervenes. In doing so, we show the close link between our basic principles of international solidarity and anti-interventionism. Together, this analysis can guide our foreign policy organizing. In this and the next chapter, we'll build on this framework. From this starting point, we'll focus on the other two of our four basic principles. In our look at U.S. policy in East Asia in this chapter, we'll consider U.S. relations with two very different neighboring countries – North Korea and China. We find in the U.S. well-worn narratives about these nations' motives and actions – often racist narratives. Many people see them as U.S. enemies – North Korea – or rivals – China. Our work in previous chapters enables us to counter and work past these narratives.

For these reasons, we'll focus less in this and the next chapter on the deeper history of East Asian (and then sub-Saharan African) politics. We won't discuss, for example, the history of leftist revolution and war in North Korea and China. These are interesting topics, especially for leftists interested in communist history. But to get at the importance of pluralism and fighting global capital, we need to move past the deeper history and into the present. In particular, we have to get at standard narratives and how those narratives fail to explain our current situation. We'll focus on more recent policy, especially policy under the Obama and Trump Administrations, and we'll use this as our background for developing a leftist path forward. A more pluralistic world will contribute to democratic reform in both North Korea and China. And it will do so without the meddling of the U.S. state. China occupies an important strategic point in the fight against global capital. Getting clear on that point will facilitate better cooperation among workers' movements.

North Korea and the Standard Narrative

The U.S. and North Korea have a contentious relationship. They've had one for years – even many Americans who don't follow world affairs know of it. The Clinton Administration behaved more carefully around North Korea, but even Clinton showed aggression. By comparison, George W. Bush threw caution to the wind. He labeled North Korea part of an 'Axis of Evil,' calling to mind the worst Cold War rhetoric. How does the U.S. press handle this? The press labels North Korea – and its leaders – as belligerent and chaotic, standing at the edge of either warfare or social collapse. I think we can summarize all this by sketching out a standard narrative about North Korea. The narrative cuts across Clinton and W. Bush Administration policy. It also covers U.S. press treatment of North Korea to this day. The standard narrative captures how many Americans see North Korea, how they think about the country and its role in the world. And so, it provides us with a useful starting point.

Here's the standard narrative about North Korea as I find it:

> *North Korea is an authoritarian hermit kingdom, and it's led by an unstable dictator. Kim Jong-un is trying to get nuclear weapons, and he's doing so in order to gain the resources his country's failed economy can't produce itself. He's holding his own citizens hostage until the world makes ransom payment, and he's not afraid to use nuclear weapons.*

The United States, on the other hand, is in a bind. It has the best intentions at heart, but it's balancing these good intentions with its national security interests. The U.S. imposes sanctions against North Korea to empower its people to replace Jong-un with democratic leadership. And the US provides aid and eases sanctions whenever Jong-un lessens his aggression.

The standard narrative lacks the status of official opinion. The White House doesn't officially publish or endorse it. Neither the press nor foreign policy experts lay it out explicitly. When he took office in January 2021, Joe Biden didn't officially endorse it. I see it as a set of background assumptions animating the views of all these groups. It holds the status of the general agreement that underlies the U.S. bipartisan foreign policy consensus as applied in North Korea. Readers should recognize that this statement flows nicely from our earlier discussion of the foreign policy consensus. Though the U.S. professes good intentions, it's really more concerned about its national security interests and policies, pursuing democracy and humanitarianism only within those terms of engagement. And then U.S. powers interpret North Korea accordingly. Republicans endorse the standard narrative, while most Democrats criticize it only at the margins. Both accept the underlying premises. The statement also captures the aggressive attitude U.S. leaders take toward North Korea. Though U.S. leaders accuse *North Korea* of aggression, *they're* the actual aggressors. U.S. rhetoric and press coverage support this conclusion. While some U.S. politicians criticized George W. Bush's 'Axis of Evil' rhetoric, they mostly accepted it. The same is true of the U.S. press.

I'll make it my goal here to capture as accurately as possible what underlies U.S. political discourse on North Korea. I'll leave it to readers to determine how closely the statement above does that. Our remaining task is to react to this discourse – to incorporate it into our politics and form our next steps with it in mind. The U.S. left must first figure what's *right* and *wrong* about it. What do U.S. politicians and the press *really* know, and what are they wrong about? And then we must form our own responses. These responses will likely look much different from the standard narrative. Our responses must effectively recognize the nuance involved, at a minimum. But – more importantly – we must redirect discussion toward the issues of pluralism and fighting global capital.

The standard narrative doesn't get everything wrong, but it comes close. Kim Jong-un *is* a totalitarian leader. In this, he follows in the tradition of his father and his grandfather. The Kim regime organizes the North Korean state and culture around a personality cult. With this in mind, the North Korean state strikes one as equal parts fascinating and appalling. In the U.S., we have an entire cottage industry of 'nonfiction' accounts of this cult and regime. The left should mostly avoid that industry, because it creates its own North Korea myths. I'd recommend a different starting point for the left: it's bad to base political systems on personality cults. And so, the standard narrative is right insofar as it points all this out. It correctly identifies the Kim regime as a totalitarian cult. But the trouble with the standard narrative is that it presents North Korean leaders as irrational or maniacal. And this presentation helps form the core assumption underlying the narrative. However, this is almost never true. In fact, North Korea behaves about as rationally as any other nation. Assuming North Korean irrationality imports various racist stereotypes about East Asian people dating back centuries. The U.S. held the same assumptions about Japanese people during World War II – that they worship absolute monarchs, and so on. It's a load of hogwash, and we should reject it.

For a more accurate and careful reading of North Korea's actions, we can draw upon the foreign policy lessons from Chapter 1. Like many nations, North Korea operates from a generally realist foreign policy. It sees the world in terms of conflict and friction between various competing powers and national interests. And it makes a frank assessment of its own power and options within that world. The North Korean regime looks at East Asia and it sees many countries more powerful than itself. It sees a neighboring country – South Korea – with which it has a history of warfare and which has a sponsor – the United States – with a great deal of power and contrary interests. In short, it knows the U.S. is the most powerful nation in the world. And it knows the U.S. sponsors nations with interests contrary to those of North Korea. It behaves accordingly. North Korea assessed the situation decades ago and concluded it should pursue nuclear weapons. It did so not to attack and conquer its neighbors. Attacking its neighbors with nuclear weapons would amount to national suicide, and North Korea bases its strategy on its own survival. It rarely dips into the kind of foolishness that would produce national suicide. Rather, North Korea pursues nuclear weapons *defensively*, as a deterrent against U.S. attack and as leverage in negotiations[182]. Among other concerns, it uses the nuclear deterrent to improve its international aid packages[183]. Particularly since the early 1990s, North Korea has needed aid in order to survive. It, again, behaves accordingly.

North Korea pursues nuclear weapons for deterrence and leverage, not for starting wars and building empires. But these aren't the only reasons. I think we can infer at least a bit beyond these main reasons. North Korean leaders probably *do* fear a U.S. invasion. Why? For one, U.S. actions in Iraq and Libya suggest as much. Most leftists already know about Iraq. In Libya, the U.S. government sponsored the overthrow of the Gaddafi regime at the precise moment the regime gave up its nuclear deterrent[184]. Kim Jong-un, of course, watched all this, and he's not a fool. Second, the U.S. already made war in Korea once. It did so in the late 1940s and early 1950s. The Kim regime in North Korea carefully cultivates memory of that war for propaganda purposes. It maintains, for example, captured U.S. military material from the earlier war, displaying it as a reminder of U.S. aggression to the North Korean people and to international visitors[185].

---

[182] In fact, this is reasonably well known even in more conservative-leaning foreign policy circles. See, for example: https://www.businessinsider.com/reason-north-korea-needs-nukes-deterrence-vs-expansion-2018-1. Last accessed: July 31, 2020.

[183] The U.S. provided significant aid to North Korea during its famine years in the 1990s. For more recent figures and discussion of international aid to North Korea, see: https://www.bbc.com/news/world-asia-48637518; https://foreignpolicy.com/2019/07/17/the-case-for-humanitarian-aid-to-north-korea/. Both last accessed: July 31, 2020.

[184] The conflict between the U.S. and Libya under Gaddafi lasted for decades, and it can't be summarized quickly. But after 9/11, Gaddafi recognized the imminent threat the U.S. posed to his government, and he began giving up his nuclear program. However, the gamble did not pay off for him. As soon as the U.S. became confident Gaddafi did not pose a credible nuclear threat, it acted to help remove him from power.

[185] North Korea maintains and displays U.S. military equipment in its Victorious War Museum in Pyongyang.

However, it reminds people of this for reasons that likely go beyond mere propaganda. It never forgets the possibility of a *real* invasion.

These things thoroughly complicate the standard U.S. narrative about North Korea. The U.S. presented that narrative most forcefully during the George W. Bush presidency, when Bush labeled North Korea a part of an 'Axis of Evil.' Many in the foreign policy mainstream – including Bill Clinton and Barack Obama – accept a less aggressive version of the narrative. But even Clinton and Obama – alleged 'progressives,' though better described as 'liberals' or 'moderates' – accept its underlying assumptions. U.S. liberals and progressives still see North Korea as the primary aggressor, despite all evidence to the contrary. And, as always, they see the U.S. as a force for peace, again despite all evidence to the contrary. These things amount to the bipartisan foreign policy consensus at work. The trouble with the consensus is that its broader narrative, too, is false. When we look at the history of U.S. and North Korean interaction, it leaves us with the inevitable conclusion that the U.S. is the main aggressor. North Korea makes mostly defensive moves. The U.S. invaded the Korean peninsula in the early 1950s. It extended its history of aggression well beyond this and into our current times. When North Korea acts aggressively now, it does so in response to the U.S. and to world events. In fact, North Korea responded to specific world events: the hunger crisis of the 1990s, the GOP victory in the 1994 U.S. Congressional elections, and George W. Bush's 'Axis of Evil' declaration in his 2002 State of the Union address. These events form the background against which North Korea pursued nuclear weapons. It reacted rationally against these events. Had the U.S. responded more effectively, it might have prevented the nuclear program. Had it not acted aggressively in the first place, there'd have been no need for one.

North Korea, then, is no irrational actor. It's not running wild, nor is it a threat to randomly attack its neighbors. A careful look at the 'hermit kingdom' reveals it as a struggling nation. It has a totalitarian leadership structure following a broadly realist foreign policy. As leftists, our discussion of U.S. policy and our responses – both in terms of international solidarity and our own policy advocacy – must take this background into account.

Trump, the Democrats, and the Narrative

Before proposing an alternative narrative, we should look at recent U.S. policy. Discussion between the Trump Administration and Democrats in Congress from 2017 to 2020 proved especially illuminating. It also put unique strains on the bipartisan foreign policy consensus. Trump originally campaigned against war – at least, he did most of the time. At other times, he issued wild nuclear threats against Iran and North Korea. Trump grounded the anti-war part of his public image in the tradition of far-right isolationism. Those views carry their own complications, tracing back to right-wing anti-Semitism in the 1930s and 1940s. Furthermore, Trump entered office in 2017 determined to oppose everything the Obama Administration did. To all appearances, this included its foreign policy moves. As a result, having Trump in office strained the bipartisan foreign policy consensus in multiple respects.

In response, Democrats doubled- and tripled-down on the foreign policy consensus. They responded to Trump by heavily deferring to the very 'experts' Trump disparaged. These experts, of course, are the people who push the consensus hardest. Democrats now adhere so rigidly to the consensus that they're its loudest articulators. This is true especially of Democratic-leaning media sources. Consider, for example, Rachel Maddow's work as a political analyst on MSNBC. When Trump ended U.S. military exercises in South Korea in June 2018, Maddow objected strongly[186]. She placed these objections into a frame of hardline, almost cartoonish adherence to foreign policy orthodoxy. And she used red-baiting rhetoric to a degree not seen since the Cold War. Maddow advocated ramping up U.S. military activity in the Korean peninsula on the explicit grounds that it would be bad for Russian president Vladimir Putin. These moves position Maddow and liberals as open, enthusiastic boosters for U.S. hegemony. By pointing this out, the U.S. left can effectively distinguish itself from liberals and progressives. It's a great case

---

[186]   https://www.msnbc.com/rachel-maddow/watch/trump-military-exercise-giveaway-to-n-korea-suits-putin-s-goals-1254434371701. Last accessed June 12, 2020.

of the sharp split on foreign policy between the socialist left and the liberal and/or progressive mainstream.

Maddow represents both a traditional approach and the tailored approach Democrats took to Trump. She captures the standard narrative above quite accurately, and she articulates very well how experts apply the standard narrative to actual events. One aspect of this, which we'll return to later, is that the standard narrative references China as much as it does North Korea itself. But, regarding North Korea, Maddow advised the U.S. to extract concessions on nuclear weapons before canceling the military exercises. This makes sense only on the assumption that North Korea pursues nuclear weapons in order to attack other nations. It works only if North Korea is planning a first strike and/or invasion of South Korea. This underlies the reasoning both of foreign policy experts and the Democratic Party as a whole. The only problem? It's a false premise, and it's false for the reasons I've outlined above. I chose Maddow as an example because she presents the argument clearly. Her argument explains Obama (and likely Biden) Administration policy in North Korea as well as the Democratic response to Trump. Had Clinton won in 2016, she'd have carried out this policy even more aggressively. As a result of those events, the U.S. would have continued its long record of bad policy in the region.

Let's, then, move on to Trump. How did Trump's policies differ from the failed consensus? Did Trump represent an improvement, a regression, or just a different way of being wrong? As we noted, Trump's policies zigzagged all over the place. This makes it difficult to interpret them, to put it mildly. With North Korea, in particular, Trump moved between bellicose rhetoric and non-interventionism. He started by carrying out an extensive Twitter feud with Kim Jong-un in 2016 and 2017. This was a foolish move opposed by practically everyone, including his own foreign policy team. Trump may have used moves like this one as negotiating tactics. But even if effective, it brings the U.S. and North Korea uncomfortably close to nuclear war for no reason other than to push the other side to the bargaining table. We might point out how obviously dangerous this is. One possible implication, which we'll explore later, is that Trump may have created a more pluralistic world *by accident*. By sufficiently damaging the U.S.'s standing with international leaders, he

152

may have turned much of the world away from U.S. influence. But it creates extraordinary risk along the way.

While feuding with Kim, Trump began threatening South Korean president Moon Jae-in. Why? He wanted to coerce South Korea into revising its existing military agreement with the U.S. That agreement established a U.S. military presence in South Korea, allowing the U.S. to use South Korea as a weapons base. It also allowed the U.S. to intimidate other regional powers, notably China and North Korea. In exchange, the U.S. provided alleged security to South Korea from allegedly hostile neighbors. South Korea also picked up the tab for some of these 'services.' As one might expect after learning about the standard narrative, U.S. foreign policy experts *love* this agreement. It's the darling of everyone aligned to the bipartisan foreign policy consensus. Experts see it as a win for everyone – the U.S. gains a new foothold for its hegemony, and South Korea gains protection from a belligerent neighbor. To foreign policy experts, this advances U.S. interests in the most effective manner possible. In the terms of mainstream U.S. foreign policy, what's not to love?

But for someone who wants to disrupt establishment thinking? Someone who (sometimes) toes a far-right, isolationist foreign policy line? It's not so great. Trump began from a stance of skepticism toward using the U.S. military to protect *any* foreign country. Add to that a bit of racism and Trump started from even greater skepticism toward South Korea. He wanted South Korea to pick up a larger portion of the tab. However, by his own terms, Trump failed miserably at this task. In response to Trump's pressure, Moon Jae-in tried to reduce hostility between the two Koreas. He thought it more fruitful to work with Kim Jong-un than with Donald Trump. After dialogue and a series of meetings, the two Koreas came closer to peace than at any point in the last 50 years. In contrast, Trump landed only a minor deal with North Korea[187]. Trump commanded headlines, but the agreement between the two Koreas stood out as the important one.

[187] For a discussion of the Singapore Agreement, see: https://www.timesofisrael.com/full-text-of-singapore-agreement-signed-by-trump-and-kim/. Last accessed June 12, 2020.

This leaves us well positioned to draw a few insights about Trump's relationship with the bipartisan foreign policy consensus. Trump aligned himself with that consensus once. Namely, he signed a major trade agreement with South Korea in 2018[188]. Foreign policy experts endorse all but the most obviously foolish of trade agreements. But, beyond this, everyone aligned to the foreign policy consensus holds Trump in utter contempt. They don't like his brinkmanship or his flirtation with nuclear war. And in the Koreas, they don't like the idea of closer relations between the North and the South. They *especially* don't like the idea if the U.S. doesn't carefully broker the relations. Why? They want to contain *China*. That's their larger goal and what they see most closely aligned to U.S. interests. They think closer relations between the Koreas – in most plausible scenarios – better serves China than it does the U.S. And they think Trump's stance wasn't helpful to U.S. interests because his plans didn't contain China in the way they want. For leftists, there's a deeper irony here. Trump challenged standard foreign policy much more strongly than any recent Democratic president. He may have thereby opened up new political space for anti-interventionism. And by weakening the U.S. on the international stage, he may have accidentally advanced pluralism in some cases. We obviously can't endorse Trump's actions in these domains. At best, he got to a positive result via the worst means possible. He irresponsibly risked nuclear war, and racism drove many of his ideas. But the situation does create certain opportunities.

Leftist Narrative on North Korea: A Starting Point

As we reflect on the current situation between the U.S. and North Korea, I think we can take a few positive steps toward forming a leftist narrative. Our narrative can serve to organize U.S. left thought and help us build new approaches. As a first step – a 101-level understanding of the relations between the U.S. and North Korea – I propose this:

---

[188] For a discussion of the trade agreement, see: https://www.businessinsider.com/trump-trade-agreement-south-korea-korus-2018-9. Last accessed June 12, 2020.

The current conflict stems from the Korean War and its aftermath, which was caused primarily by U.S. aggression. The U.S. is currently a hegemonic or imperialist occupying power in South Korea and the primary impediment to peace. Its apparent intentions are grounded in national interest: it wants to maintain domination of East Asia and limit Chinese power and reach. Trump's rather incompetent bungling of the situation has, ironically, pushed the North and South Koreans closer to peace. On balance, the conflict was probably in better shape in early 2019 under Trump than it would've been under a Hillary Clinton presidency.

I think this should both inform and surprise us. It shows, in particular, the gap between liberals and progressives, on the one hand, and the U.S. left, on the other. It should count as a warning to U.S. leftists about Democrats and the Democratic Party. Namely, it warns us that Democratic politicians are generally opposed to a good leftist foreign policy. Any electoralist movement on the U.S. left – particularly one operating after the 2016 and 2020 losses of Bernie Sanders – should be aware of this gap. The Democratic Party is no ally on these issues. And any process of convincing it to change its attitudes has barely begun. In certain cases – and in certain respects – the Democratic Party operates to the right of Trump and Trumpists on foreign policy. As leftists, we must weigh the merits of persuading Democrats versus starting from scratch. We'll build our leftist consensus around new ideas, motivated by different class interests and groups.

China

Let's start with one of China's unique features. Unlike most of our previous cases, the U.S. doesn't often station troops in China[189]. The U.S. does not occupy China, and China's current government began in part as a reaction against U.S. – and later Soviet – hegemony in the 1940s. At times, the U.S. takes an adversarial stance toward China. And the U.S. remains the ally of a Chinese rival state on the island of Taiwan. But the

---

[189] At least, the U.S. doesn't often station troops in China *recently*. It has a history of military interventionism in China, but that history plays out mostly in the late 19th and early 20th century.

U.S. takes these stances with a degree of wariness and respect. It recognizes China as a growing power and player on the regional and world stage. Thus, economic and political issues drive the relationship between the U.S. and China. Economic development, the expansion of capitalist markets, and the global supply chain all loom large on the horizon. This produces a testy situation where the U.S. holds China responsible for low wages, low quality goods, and other problems in the U.S. related to wages and working conditions. And yet the U.S. *depends* on China due to China's growing role in the supply chain. Combined with globalization writ large, this situation produces challenges for the U.S. system and for the left. Right-wing U.S. demagogues, in particular, manipulate attitudes toward China in order to claim to take the interests of working-class Americans to heart.

This brings us to Donald Trump and Trumpist rhetoric on China, and Trump didn't disappoint. More than perhaps any other politician, Trump leaned in to this approach. He often discussed China in the context of global trade. He kept it as a theme, even though he transformed the details from the beginning of his campaign through the end of his presidency. It thereby remained core to Trump's brand, but his statements ranged from absurd to semi-coherent. For a taste of the former, see for example the way Trump pronounces the word 'China[190].' He manages to combine menacing, threatening sounds with comical ones, giving the word a hard 'Ch' sound and leaving us at a loss whether to take him very seriously or not seriously at all. He also labeled China a currency manipulator, claiming it engages in unfair trade practices. At one point, he even accused China of 'raping' the U.S. via its trade policy[191]. He thus combined the racist with the absurd in a way unique to his own brand of politics.

Let's focus on how this situation arose – one where Trump peddled baloney and tried to make it stick. The U.S. left can learn from it. For one, it tells us a great deal about the role of economic development and resources in foreign policy. We'll discuss that topic in even more detail in the next chapter, where we'll review U.S.-Nigeria relations and how these

---

[190] See: https://www.youtube.com/watch?v=RDrfE9I8_hs. Last accessed: July 31, 2020.
[191] See: https://www.bbc.com/news/election-us-2016-36185012. Last accessed: July 31, 2020.

relations represent our broader economic approach to sub-Saharan Africa. But for now, we'll discuss how it plays out in leftist movements and the global supply chain. It also tells us a great deal about building a more pluralistic world. China will be a major part of any pluralistic world. It's an emerging power that could become an even more important regional power. It could balance U.S. power both in East Asia and on the world stage.

Obama, Trump, and Trade

Trump didn't toss baloney randomly into the void. He sensed weakness and pounced on the opportunity. In fact, he made Democratic weakness on global trade central to his political brand. He built this brand with his expansive media platform: shows like *The Apprentice*, extensive interviews, and even his character in WWE professional wrestling. In the early days, he also had no political responsibilities, opening up possibilities for him to tweet all day from the sidelines with no repercussions. And he could complain about Obama's policy moves without needing to *do* anything about it. The U.S. left should treat all this as a great example of a certain rhetorical strategy. We find the strategy among political groups looking to defend the interests common to domestic and global capital. When he spoke about these issues, Trump spoke *about* and *to* entirely *different* groups of people. For example, he might speak *about* the American worker, but while doing so he does *not* speak *to* the American worker. He chooses a different audience for the message. In this example, Trump speaks *to* people who *falsely* think of themselves as American workers – people who identify with the American worker aesthetically or culturally[192].

Consider, for example, Trump's claim in late 2016 that he 'saved' 1,000 jobs at Carrier Corp. in Indiana. Trump claimed he prevented Carrier from moving these jobs to Mexico. His basis for the claim? Carrier retained about 700 jobs in Indiana for a time after previously announcing a plan to move production to Mexico. Is this how things happened? Well, no[193].

---

[192] I cover this topic extensively in my broader treatment of Trump and Trumpism. See Drabek 2020.

[193] https://www.popularmechanics.com/technology/infrastructure/a20066498/carrier-factory-donald-trump-jobs/. Last accessed June 16, 2020.

Carrier did move some of those 700 jobs, and they eventually laid off hundreds of people[194]. Maybe Trump *temporarily* helped some fraction of those 700 workers and their families. But those workers knew perfectly well Trump's actions and statements were largely symbolic. They knew Trump tailored his statements for a different audience, and their union president said as much. But Trump wasn't talking *to* the workers at Carrier. He was merely talking *about* them. Trump was talking *to* people who identify with the manufacturing sector but aren't blue-collar workers in the industry. This includes people like: foremen and managers, senior executives, other people who identify culturally with blue-collar work but do not themselves perform blue-collar work, people who live in the town but don't work for Carrier, people who live in other manufacturing towns, and others. The only blue-collar workers who make up part of Trump's audience for this are, perhaps, *retired* blue-collar workers. For retired workers, this all might be closer to a memory rather than a daily, lived experience. They may not retain the kind of direct experience needed to see through Trump's lies.

This distinction between audience and subject allows Trump to subvert the truth in new ways. It allows him to get away with shrouding the class interests of the wealthy in the jargon of the working class. Indeed, this right-wing strategy goes back to the time of Ronald Reagan, if not earlier. Trump merely honed it for a new era. For its part, the U.S. left must monitor this rhetoric. But we must also develop our own alternative narrative of how the U.S. economy impacts working-class life. We can't cede the field to people like Trump. Nor can we abandon working-class people in the way Democrats do. And, to be clear, Obama and Democrats abandon working-class people *brazenly*. They make little show of offering them *any* kind of political vision. But even more progressive Democrats like Elizabeth Warren do the same things. They run on better platforms than Obama, et al., but they still show massive unfriendliness – even borderline contempt or hostility – to working-class people and working-class interests.

---

[194] See: https://www.reuters.com/article/us-usa-trump-carrier/more-layoffs-at-indiana-factory-trump-made-deal-to-keep-open-idUSKBN1F02TL. Last accessed June 16, 2020.

As president, Trump had to translate some of this messaging into policy. In other words, he had to actually *do* something. His policy never held together well, but we can take away at least some lessons for what this rhetoric looks like in practice. We see here the damaging effects of anti-immigrant rhetoric of the kinds we discussed in Chapter 3. We also see the damaging effects of anti-Chinese fearmongering, racist tirades, right-wing ideas on global trade, and so on. Trump repeatedly used tariffs, for example, in a way that combined all these things and shrouded them in pseudo-concern for working-class Americans. How did Trump do this? He said he would use tariffs to displace China from its role in the global supply chain. And we can broadly distinguish between two phases in Trump's tariff strategy. The first was a round of tariffs in 2017-2018. And the second was his coronavirus-flavored re-election campaign in 2020. In practice, in both these phases Trump used tariffs to nudge or coerce companies to stop making products in China or using Chinese parts for their products.

In the first phase – the one in 2017-2018 – Trump imposed tariffs on a broad collection of Chinese goods[195]. Even the term 'broad' treats Trump too kindly. We could better describe the list of Chinese goods the tariffs cover as 'arbitrary' or 'random.' In response, China imposed much more strategic tariffs on the U.S. It's unclear whether either side's actions had large impact[196], though if anyone 'won' the tariff war it was probably China. Aside from rising aluminum and steel prices, there was no large-scale impact on either country. The tariffs did, however, hurt U.S. farmers, particularly soybean farmers. They probably cost Trump some support in places like Iowa, though he still carried the state in the 2020 election. And some companies – notably Harley Davidson and Ford – moved production or canceled imports to avoid the tariffs. The tariffs did not benefit American workers as a class, at least in no way worth the costs. But that's not necessarily a problem for Trump. As we saw earlier, he wasn't 'hurting

---

[195] See, for example, https://www.businessinsider.com/trump-trade-war-tariffs-effect-on-economy-prices-consumer-stocks-2018-7 for a collection of the goods covered. Last accessed June 16, 2020.

[196] See, for example, https://www.politifact.com/article/2018/jul/30/effects-donald-trumps-trade-war/. Last accessed June 16, 2020.

his base.' American workers and small farmers were not Trump's base, and they're not the base of the U.S. right wing. Trump grounded his political support in, e.g., higher income managers in the manufacturing industry.

In the second phase, Trump took a much more multi-lateral approach. It's here where the Trump Administration became less ham-handed and showed potential policy innovation. Starting in early 2020, Trump pursued possible action against China that involved other regional governments. For example, Trump officials spoke about forming an 'Economic Prosperity Network[197].' The goal of such a network would have been to balance China's role in the global supply chain. Of course, for the moment, all this talk is hypothetical. There is no 'Economic Prosperity Network,' and there are no longer any immediate prospects for creating one after Trump's loss. But someone – perhaps even Joe Biden or the Democrats – may pick up the pieces and run with it. Global capital always looks for ways to promote international solidarity among capitalists. The left must do so among *workers*. The bottom line for the left is that many Americans are hurting. The left lacks a unified, international message for how to make sense of that hurt and how to unite to stop it. The Democrats remain uninterested in addressing the situation. They write off working-class Americans of all races as voters they can't win, and their platform often starkly opposes working-class interests. As a result of these developments, Trump found and exploited an opportunity. Right-wingers will continue trying to exploit it.

This situation creates opportunities for the U.S. left. The left can put together a narrative where the Democrats cannot or will not. And it can build and maintain grassroots power to share that narrative and build movements. The left can certainly put together a narrative that moves beyond the nativism and racism of people like Trump or Biden. Indeed, *only* the left can put together this kind of narrative. Only the left offers to suffering people a path showing where their interests come together and

---

[197] https://www.reuters.com/article/us-health-coronavirus-usa-china/trump-administration-pushing-to-rip-global-supply-chains-from-china-officials-idUSKBN22G0BZ. Last accessed June 16, 2020.

how their interests stand opposed to those of business. We can build a new kind of class collaboration – one between workers, tenants, and other oppressed and marginalized people. We rarely see this kind of coalition in the U.S. To develop this further, let's take a look at China's role in the global economy. We'll use this case to apply our basic principles of pluralism and fighting global capital.

China as Economic Power and Regional Hegemon

Over the course of the last seven decades, China grew from a small, developing state into a regional hegemon and burgeoning world power. It did so at first through a communist revolution and the nationalization of private industry. After the death of Mao Zedong, it did so through centralized, controlled market reforms[198]. In light of its sharp turn toward capitalist development in the 1970s and 1980s, China now occupies a huge role in the supply chains of U.S. companies. It's difficult to overstate the size and scope of this role. At a broad level, China handles massive amounts of production and assembly work for the products of U.S. companies. It handles work from the mass production that might come to mind all the way to work for high-tech companies like Apple[199]. Its manufacturing industry tends to specialize in handling work that companies based in other nations have already standardized. Companies using manufacturing tools like Lean production and just-in-time inventory – tools once primarily used in the context of Japanese or U.S. domestic production lines – now focus on Chinese industry.

Many people already understand the role Chinese manufacturing plays in the world economy. At least, they grasp the big picture, if not the details. But far fewer people pay attention to the role China plays in consumer markets. China now has a *huge* population – around 1.5 billion

---

[198] There's obviously far more to be said about China's revolutionary period and its turn toward capitalism. For an overview highly accessible and relevant to new socialists, I'd recommend the discussion in Sunkara 2019, pp. 131-153.

[199] The U.S. International Trade Commission provided a helpful overview in a 2009 report. https://www.brookings.edu/wp-content/uploads/2012/05/DeanFungExplainingChinaspositionintheGlobalSupplyChain.pdf. Last accessed June 17, 2020.

people. As it develops and builds more internal wealth, China concentrates income at the top and – to some degree – in the middle. While many Chinese people remain impoverished, even a small part of 1.5 billion adds up to millions and millions of people buying luxury goods and other consumer products. For this reason, U.S. companies increasingly market their goods to the Chinese market. Consider the U.S. film industry. As little as 30-40 years ago, the U.S. film industry ignored China and focused mostly on the domestic market. Even as little as 15-20 years ago, Chinese consumers played only a marginal role. By 2020, China surged to one of the world's largest film markets. It's now arguably the world's most important, aside from the U.S. itself. U.S. film companies even approve or cancel films based on how well they'll do in China. And the Chinese state – through its powers of censorship and regulation – plays an outsized role in this process. Occasionally this works to the detriment of the free expression of ideas[200]. Chinese investors also play an increasingly large role in the economics of film production and distribution. China thereby now heavily engages in the film industry in all its parts – from conception to production to distribution.

The size of the Chinese economy and its newfound role on the world stage drives these forces. China now has the world's second largest economy measured purely by GDP[201]. And if we switch from GDP to the purchasing power of its currency, it has the world's largest[202]. However, we shouldn't exaggerate, as racist fearmongers in the U.S. do. China has about five times more people than the U.S. Given this fact, the U.S. economy is still much larger *per person*. China also invests in economic sectors likely to freeze this relationship in place for some time. But, by any measure, the Chinese economy is *huge*, and increasingly so. At the same time, Chinese development has led to spikes in inequality. Quickly

---

[200] Martha Bayles documents in The Atlantic some of the issues of censorship arising from recent Chinese state regulator attitudes – and changed in attitude – toward popular films. https://www.theatlantic.com/ideas/archive/2019/09/hollywoods-great-leap-backward-free-expression/598045/. Last accessed June 17, 2020.

[201] https://en.wikipedia.org/wiki/List_of_countries_by_GDP_(nominal). Last accessed: July 31, 2020.

[202] https://en.wikipedia.org/wiki/List_of_countries_by_GDP_(PPP). Last accessed: July 31, 2020.

transforming the country from a rural, agricultural state to a manufacturing power resulted in various side-effects – inequality among them. China massively displaced people from the land, marshaling together a new urban workforce. We saw in our discussion of Syria some of the results of this kind of state-led proletarianization. Among other things, it breeds popular resentment. The Chinese state's long history of Marxist and Maoist rhetoric compounds these problems. It's jarring to hear a state preach class politics and collective action, on the one hand, while impoverishing people and displacing them from the land, on the other. China carefully laid the groundwork for this transition over a period of many years, but the memory of Marxist and Maoist principles remains among many within the country. And, also like Syria, the style and pace of development in China encourage creeping authoritarianism in its domestic politics.

This provides the U.S. left with the background needed to understand recent news from China and to interpret news moving forward. In 2018, the National People's Congress, China's highest legislative body, voted to eliminate term limits for President Xi Jinping[203]. Along with doing so, it placed Xi's name and official ideology in the Chinese Communist Party constitution. While there are various complexities involved with such a move, it's tantamount to placing Xi Jinping alongside Mao and others in the pantheon of Chinese communism. None of these steps actually guarantee that Xi Jinping will be a president for life. Indeed, the Chinese state responds more closely to public demand than the U.S. press thinks. But it represents a sharp turn toward greater authoritarianism and the closest China has come in decades to having an official personality cult. Thus, the U.S. left should treat cases like China less as random instances of politics gone wrong and more as the predictable consequences of certain kinds of capitalist economics. Putting in place a more democratic economic system – or democratizing the systems already in place – will tend to produce better politics. This is as true in China as it is in the U.S.

As I noted previously, a great deal of uncertainty remains in the Chinese domestic political system. The Chinese state is responsive to public

---

[203] https://www.bbc.com/news/world-asia-china-43361276. Last accessed June 17, 2020.

demand, even though it – as with most countries – actively manipulates that demand. There's also remaining resistance to Xi Jinping, even within the Chinese state itself. We might combine these facts with the inherent uncertainty involved in China's development plan. Sharp twists and turns in the success of that development might also produce changes in the Chinese state. But, overall, the trend toward authoritarianism is a noticeable one. It would be highly productive for the left to think in greater detail – and put on the discussion table – a comparison between the kind of creeping authoritarianism found in China with the kinds found in places like Brazil, India, Russia, and the U.S. itself.

China, the U.S., and the Basic Principles

American discourse on China displays distrust at best and racism at worst. Some Americans worry China will 'take over' the world economy and dominate the U.S. This is racist fearmongering, but it plays a large role in U.S. politics. We find this most prominently in right-wing politics, especially Trump and Trumpist rhetoric. That's hardly surprising. But it doesn't drive just the right wing. We also find it driving broader U.S. political narratives. Joe Biden ran a racist anti-China ad shortly after becoming the likely 2020 Democratic nominee[204], and his campaign remained friendly to racist anti-China rhetoric. The U.S. left should obviously reject these kinds of racist narratives, a rejection that offers another way for the left to distinguish itself from the rest of U.S. politics, even including liberal Democrats. We need to strongly oppose racism, especially the kind grounded in nationalism. In our current political climate, we should note what happens when U.S. politicians take racist remarks to broader audiences. Racist or foolish remarks appear differently when we pull them from their intended viewers and place them in front of a well-informed or international public. Consider, for example, the speech Donald Trump made to the U.N. in September 2018[205]. He stated that "in less than 2 years, my administration has accomplished more than

---

[204]https://inthesetimes.com/article/22538/biden-trump-china-racism-asian-american-groups-military-pivot-covid. Last accessed June 17, 2020.
[205] https://www.youtube.com/watch?v=VDPd5wOaBOU. Last accessed June 17, 2020.

almost any administration in the history of our country." The audience laughed at him. Why? Well-informed world leaders made up the audience. Circumstances force them to understand the U.S. deeply, and they knew Trump's remarks were baloney. Trump assumed, to the contrary, that since they lead *different* countries they wouldn't understand *his*.

As a matter of fact, China has a long, long way to go before it displaces the U.S. as the world hegemon. The left can thus easily point out the key lie of racist nationalism. In the short-term, China can mildly disrupt U.S. hegemony and advance a more pluralistic world at the margins. This carries some benefits, benefits we should consider. China might balance U.S. power in East Asia and the Pacific. It could thereby relieve some countries of U.S. domination and pressure, freeing them to take bolder, more democratic steps. The U.S. left should carefully encourage these trends, but it shouldn't do so uncritically. Indeed, we should stay aware of certain long-term dangers. China's growing influence on international markets and governments goes hand-in-hand with authoritarian tendencies in its own domestic politics. Thus, as China becomes more powerful, it will carry the problems of any powerful nation. This remained largely a domestic concern when China was a minor power, but it now plays an increasingly international role. Authoritarian tendencies – both domestically and in terms of its foreign policy – compose some of the major reasons to oppose the U.S.'s international influence. We may one day oppose China's influence for the same reason. As readers should recall from Chapters 1 and 2, the U.S. hardly has a monopoly on problematic uses of power. Free speech and expression stand out as one area of concern worth watching in the case of China.

We find a world system with competing influences and changing relations among nations. We should take from this the lesson that we need greater pluralism in the world system. Pluralism remains the only force offering people space for organizing more democratic systems in their own countries. It frees them from the dominance of nations like the U.S. – or China – dominance that often includes election interference or coercion. Hegemons threaten genuine democracy everywhere. Our second lesson from China is that we must include the entire global supply chain under the banner of 'fighting global capitalism.' We might think we can fight our labor battles 'locally.' But these battles often grow over deep international roots. Those roots run through countries with economies based in the manufacturing of basic goods or extraction of natural resources. Many U.S. companies work with China as one such country. We'll look at another case of this in the following chapter on sub-Saharan Africa, where Nigeria stands out as another nation with this kind of relationship with the U.S. and U.S. companies. Companies wage labor battles partly through threats to outsource work. Most U.S. workers understand this component quite well. But companies also *shift* work, distributing and conducting it within different parts of their own existing supply chains[206].

Our four basic principles work together in tandem in these labor battles. Fighting global capital begins with international solidarity. And – as we see from the case of China – we must build that solidarity among workers across global supply chains. By promoting anti-interventionism and pluralism, we open up space for movements in other countries to build the organizations that will be a part of international solidarity campaigns. These steps operate as a feedback loop. By building initial, tentative bonds of international solidarity, the U.S. left and labor movements will grasp in greater detail *why* it must promote anti-interventionism and pluralism. It thus reinforces and intensifies its own movements. These steps result, in the long-term, in an effective fight against global capitalism.

---

[206] On this point, see especially Moody 2017. Moody points out the ways changes in capitalist development open up new opportunities for organizing.

Chapter 7

Sub-Saharan Africa

U.S. foreign policy discussion frequently shortchanges Africa in its treatment of world events. What holds here for Africa as a continent holds even more for sub-Saharan Africa as a region. On the rare occasion the U.S. press does discuss Africa as headline news, it tends to discuss North Africa in the context of Mediterranean or Middle Eastern politics. We might point to the deep history of U.S. racism and anti-blackness as one cause. Our standard foreign policy narrative also focuses on troops in active deployment or nations the U.S. sees as rivals. This stands out as a second cause – with only a few notable exceptions, the U.S. tends not to deploy troops to sub-Saharan Africa on a regular basis. The U.S. relationship with sub-Saharan Africa tends to take on different forms. Indeed, we'll focus on these different forms in this chapter. They'll prove especially instructive for the U.S. left.

In another sense, we ought to be surprised sub-Saharan Africa gets so little attention in the U.S. press and narrative of world events. The region plays a critical role in the U.S. economy and the international economy, and it played an even larger role in U.S. history. Readers surely know about this history, since it relates to a dark period of oppression and slavery. Even today, the relationship remains one of extraction and exploitation. And perhaps that's *why* our narratives don't focus on the region. Discussion tends to cover over the underlying economic basis for international political relationships. In particular, sub-Saharan Africa is a major source of resources and a haven for capital. Furthermore, the U.S.

in general – and African-Americans in particular – played a key role in the development of sub-Saharan Africa. While we may choose from many examples, two cases stand out. In the first case – that of Liberia – a U.S.-based settlement project literally founded the country. The U.S. created the settlement project – the American Colonization Society – in response to the growing population of free black Americans in the early 19th century[207]. The U.S. state – long comfortable with black Americans in slavery – feared the existence of black Americans in a state of freedom. Free black Americans and abolitionist communities – both black and white – criticized the ACS on these grounds. More recent discussions of Liberia present the founding of the nation in a better light. Liberia's own founding myths do so in particular. But leftist groups largely read the episode as a case of U.S. capital attempting to discard a former slave population. It no longer needed large numbers of people as slavery receded.

Our second case is that of Ghanaian liberation in the mid-20th century. After World War II, Ghana turned the tide in its independence struggle against the remains of the British Empire. In its liberation movement, it searched for bonds of international solidarity. And it found those bonds with African-Americans. Indeed, no less a figure than W. E. B. Du Bois participated in the movement at the behest of Kwame Nkrumah, a major leader. Nkrumah serves as a key example of socialism in an African context, and readers looking for a case of socialism in a developing nation ought to consult this case[208]. After being labeled a communist by the U.S. and persecuted for it, Du Bois became so disillusioned with the U.S. he *moved* to Ghana. He lived the final years of his life in the newly liberated nation.

I'll focus on Nigeria in this chapter. In many ways it well represents the U.S. approach to sub-Saharan Africa. What's that approach? The U.S. tried

---

[207] On the history of black resistance to the American Colonization Society, see Power-Greene 2014.

[208] There's an extensive primary and secondary literature discussion on Du Bois's experience in Ghana, and we don't have time to do justice to it here. Readers looking for a start can see: https://www.thedailybeast.com/how-web-du-bois-found-his-final-resting-place-in-ghana. Last accessed: July 31, 2020.

to form careful, deep alliances with nations after they overthrew European colonial rule. It first posed itself as an anti-colonial power, as we discussed earlier in Chapter 2 with regard to Woodrow Wilson. But this changed as it reworked these relationships in a Cold War context. In the Cold War, the U.S. competed with the Soviet Union for the allegiance of each nation. And the Soviets posed themselves more successfully as an anti-colonial power. When nations chose the U.S., they tended to build relationships in economic terms, with global capital dominating the landscape. Capital facilitated relationships, and it did so increasingly with the support of U.S. nonprofits and non-governmental organizations (NGOs). U.S. military action was relatively rare, for a number of reasons. The possibility of war with the Soviet Union loomed, and the Soviets integrated any U.S. military action into an anti-colonial critique. These social forces sometimes deterred the U.S. from sending troops. We did see, of course, various exceptions. But Nigeria exemplified all these features. We'll see in Nigeria – as we see in much of sub-Saharan Africa – the importance of global capital. It all shows why the U.S. left must take fighting global capital as a key goal of its foreign policy.

Unlike previous chapters, we'll focus in this chapter on only a single nation as a key example. This is not because the region is any less important than the others. On the contrary, it illustrates key economic principles of U.S. foreign policy better than any other region. To get at these principles, we'll go into more depth on Nigeria in some respects. We'll also cover some of the basic economic terms and forces driving U.S. relations in the region. Sticking to one example will allow us to go into a greater depth on these issues than we achieved with the other regions. These economic terms will broaden our horizons as leftists and enable us to do more analytical work. And so, we begin with these underlying forces in order to expand our toolkit. This initial discussion will clarify a long-term goal of a leftist foreign policy – preparing for the fight against global capital.

Primitive Accumulation and Extractivism

Before we look at the case of Nigeria, let's discuss major forces driving broader U.S. policy in the region. These forces form much of the substance of our discussion. We'll find that the U.S. left already has important tools to put to work in discussing relations between the U.S. and sub-Saharan Africa. In particular, we hold the analytical tool of primitive accumulation and related concepts.

'Primitive accumulation' as a tool of leftist analysis dates to Karl Marx's analysis of capitalism in the three volumes of Capital and other works. Marx's concept serves a specific role in the leftist analysis of capitalist history. Marx describes capitalism as a system of value-in-motion. The capitalist begins with the various tools, equipment, raw materials, etc. needed for the production of goods and services. Marx calls these things 'constant capital.' The capitalist then hires workers and pays them according to the value of their labor-power, i.e., the value of their ability to produce value. The value for which the capitalist compensates workers Marx calls 'variable capital.' However, workers produce for the capitalist a value *greater* than the value of their labor power. The difference between these two values – the worker's labor power and what the worker actually produces – is what Marx calls 'surplus-value.' The capitalist thus builds profits by selling goods at a price higher than they pay for constant and variable capital. Surplus-value allows the system to continue in a giant cycle. Capitalists make profits, and then they invest those profits in new constant and variable capital, and so on in an endless generation of value and profit[209].

And yet a puzzle remains. How did capitalists get the *original* value? How did they acquire the original constant and variable capital needed to set the system in motion? We have a chicken-and-egg problem at the bottom of the system. In our modern economy, there's no issue here at all. The credit system answers these questions[210]. Capitalists take out loans to start businesses, buy the necessary equipment, and so on. Even without formal credit, they have other potential sources. But the credit system didn't operate in this way at the *beginning* of the capitalist system.

---

[209] As an overview of Marxist analysis of capital, this remains necessarily very incomplete. See, of course, Marx 1990 [1867]. But readers looking to work through this material should also consult Harvey 2010.

[210] Marx moves on to these issues in Volume 2 of Capital. See Marx 1992 [1885] and Harvey 2013.

Classical economists didn't really answer these questions. Even when they did, they trotted out silly foundation myths no historian or philosopher takes seriously. Some claimed, for example, that early capitalists simply worked hard and built up the wealth. For us, that's a non-starter. Marx, on the other hand, had a defensible answer. He cited primitive accumulation as the source of original capital.

What's involved in primitive accumulation[211]? It incorporates many different sources of wealth. A few early capitalists built wealth through using the feudal rent system to extract rent money from rural farmers. Others robbed property and wealth from churches or state institutions. In some cases, they explicitly stole it, while in other cases they extorted it. Some capitalists acted with a high level of subtlety. They closed off public commons and resources and claimed the land for themselves. And yet other capitalists acted with no subtlety at all. They fought and killed neighbors, taking their land. Or they drove the state to invade and colonize people in other nations. One key force of primitive accumulation is what analysts of capitalism call 'proletarianization' – or the forced conversion of people into wage workers. Early capitalists, for example, displaced farmers from their land, seized the land for building wealth, and forced the farmers to move to cities. In cities, farmers then became wage laborers in order to survive. And – far from least in importance – capitalists turned to racialized slavery. This played a role in many places, but it played one of the largest roles in the U.S. Americans kidnapped Africans and invented an entire system of racial classification to justify their enslavement[212]. In short, capitalists *stole* the wealth needed to start the cycle of accumulation. And they stole it in many ways. This process of theft is what we call primitive accumulation.

But accumulation didn't stop with the original building of wealth. We see it today in 'non-primitive' forms. It didn't stop after slavery ended or

---

[211] Marx ends Volume 1 of Capital with his analysis of primitive accumulation. See Marx 1990 [1867], pp. 873-940.

[212] One very common myth in discussion of race in America is the idea that racist beliefs or racial bias comes first, and then mistreatment comes second. But this reverses the order. In fact, the enslavement of certain people came prior to their racialization. See Kendi 2017 for discussion of this point.

the U.S. spread to the Pacific Ocean (and beyond). Capitalists still accumulate wealth today in similar ways. In our current era of financial capitalism, capitalists accumulate through new systems of grift and grifters. They privatize public resources, like natural resources and home utilities. They push for tax breaks and other forms of corporate welfare. They create shell companies to transfer resources from taxpayers to their own pockets. And they even expand these schemes to include nonprofits and public-private partnerships. Capitalists charge rents, interest, user fees, late fees, transaction fees, service fees, and so on. They conjure all manner of invented methods of generating profits without creating anything of actual value.

Marxist geographer David Harvey called these newer forms 'accumulation by dispossession'[213]. He put a novel theoretical structure around them. These systems look like primitive accumulation in many ways, and they serve similar functions. But they take on a more expansive role in the capitalist system. They operate not at its early stages, but also in advanced stages and in relationships between more and less advanced capitalist nations. These ongoing forms of accumulation serve to perpetuate divisions of race, et al. But – more to the point of our discussion – they also drive U.S. foreign policy with less developed capitalist nations. And so, these kinds of accumulation explain not only the *origin* of wealth but also a large part of the *persistence* of wealth over time.

Other theorists point to 'extractivism' as a relevant term of analysis for some of these activities. And in some cases we'll find this an equally useful term for leftist analysis of U.S. policy in the region. This term refers to the extraction of natural resources or raw materials from the land. While it can refer to any such extraction, it typically refers to extraction for export to other nations. In fact, extraction occurs in almost every nation in the world. But it takes on particular importance when considering the relationship between the developing world and the U.S. and Europe. European nations and the U.S. continue to this day to engage in extractivist policies, and they've developed new ways to do it.

---

[213] See Harvey 2018 [1982].

Increasingly, we see extraction of resources mediated directly by transnational corporations with little direct state involvement. We also see – and will see, in the case of Nigeria – extraction mediated by NGOs and nonprofits rather than by the state. New developments in extractivist policies and other forms of capital accumulation point our leftist movements in new directions. They show the necessity of fighting global capital at each of its points of impact. But they also show the need to develop new, responsive ways of fighting global capital. Nonetheless, extractivism presents unique challenges and dangers to leftist movements. The extraction of resources – from mining in Bolivia to oil in Alaska – creates divisions within leftist movements. It especially creates divisions between labor-focused and environmental-focused sections of our movements. We must carefully negotiate these challenges[214].

Nigeria From Dictatorship to the All Progressives Congress

The U.S. has stationed troops and fought wars in sub-Saharan Africa. Despite the lack of headlines, it never entirely avoided this part of its standard foreign policy menu. But these things play a smaller role in U.S. policy in sub-Saharan Africa than its policy in the Middle East. They play a smaller role in Nigeria, in particular[215]. Economic and security issues dominate the foreign policy discussion in Nigeria. In recent years, we've

---

[214] While extractivism is a major issue in Africa, it's also an issue in many other parts of the world. See Riofrancos 2020 for an in-depth discussion of extractivism in Ecuador. She especially focuses on the point that the extraction of resources can divide leftists. In the case of Ecuador, she contrasts the more nationalistic, labor-oriented leftism of Ecuador's leaders to the more environmental-focused leftism of Indigenous groups in the country. See also Veltmeyer and Petras 2014 for a broader discussion of extractivism throughout Latin America. The essays in Veltmeyer and Petras's collection distinguish in particular between 'classical extractivism' and a 'new extractivism' where the state retakes partial control of the process. Developments in Nigeria are much closer to classical extractivism than new extractivism.

[215] To be clear, the role is small, but it's not zero. In fact, the U.S. does station troops in Nigeria and also other parts of West Africa. Those troops have done some of the activities associated with U.S. troop presence in other places, such as accompanying Nigerian forces on anti-drug and counterterrorism operations as recently as April 2020. See, for example, https://www.nytimes.com/2020/04/18/world/africa/west-africa-special-operations-medevac.html. Last accessed June 18, 2020. The overall theme of U.S. troops presence in West Africa tends to be that it's relatively small, temporary, and targeted.

seen U.S.-based NGOs and other actors take on a role as large as that of the U.S. state. Perhaps even as large a role – on the surface – as that of global capital. To get at this background, we'll start by examining recent internal politics in Nigeria. Nigeria's transition from a military dictatorship to a representative democracy tells much of the story here, particularly how the Nigerian state entered into deep relationships with these global forces. And it tells us why internal resistance within Nigeria remains so difficult. Official electoral channels in Nigeria remain deeply embedded within the system of global capital.

Nigeria's 1993 presidential election marked the beginning of its transition from military dictatorship to representative democracy. After a decade of direct military rule, the military regime decided an election would add 'stability' (in the senses we discussed earlier) to the system. And so, it planned and held an election. The need to transition to an electoral system thereby arose less from external pressure than from internal forces. Indeed, the U.S. applied little external pressure to its Nigerian military allies. The U.S. foreign policy establishment, of course, made all the usual noises about 'democracy.' But it never fully gave up its friendly relations with the regime. Ronald Reagan, in particular, laid out the blueprint for the standard U.S. response, routinely expressing 'concern' without showing any real *concern* about the situation[216]. The U.S. slapped Nigeria with economic sanctions, but these were light and never came with follow up action. And so, the Nigerian military held an election, but it held a limited one. Though it began with *some* good intentions, the election degenerated quickly.

Ultimately, the military didn't like the results of the election. A party it deemed unacceptable won. In response, it buried those results and installed a different leader. How did all this happen? Unofficial results showed a victory by Moshood Abiola of the Social Democratic Party (SDP). The SDP positioned itself electorally as a center-left political party. It checked in as more liberal than social democratic or socialist according to how we laid out these terms in Chapter 1. But even a liberal program

---

[216]https://www.washingtonpost.com/archive/politics/1985/08/28/military-ousts-government-of-nigeria/a796b3f5-46d4-40a1-a081-e071475e6cba/. Last accessed June 18, 2020.

strained the tolerance level of the Nigerian military. The military wanted a gradual transition rather than a sharp break from the current system, but it thought the SDP would break with the system more sharply than it was prepared to allow.

Abiola himself was a businessman. He represented no obvious threat to the nation's existing economic and political structure. Perhaps – as the Nigerian military may have thought – electing a liberal would lead to social democracy or socialism down the road. But Abiola's campaign showed no signs of this. He campaigned on issues of poverty relief combined with fiscal caution, even dipping into outright fiscal conservatism. And so, his program did not extend beyond making capitalism a bit less painful for people. Nor do we find any reason to believe he would have made an ally to any socialist groups in the region. His fear of the Nigerian military and the U.S. outweighed any hint of movement in that direction. Furthermore, given the recent dissolution of the Soviet Union, Cold War politics did not loom on the horizon in the way they would have a decade prior. Our remaining conclusion, then, is the one with which we began. The Nigerian military wanted a gradual transition program where it remained largely in control. It would not tolerate even minor deviation in the early stages of that transition.

The Nigerian military voided the results of the election. Indeed, it didn't even bother releasing the results. In response, Abiola sought help from the U.S. and the U.K. He likely did so because those nations still took a rhetorical stance in favor of democracy, and Abiola presented a threat neither to democracy nor to the underlying interests of global capital in Nigeria. But the U.S. and U.K. did not provide assistance. The Nigerian military did, however, turn the country over to civilian rule rather than immediately to the military dictatorships of old. A corporate executive – Ernest Shonekan – led the government for about 3 months. Sani Abacha, a general and former Minister of Defense, overthrew Shonekan in another military coup. Abacha based his 5-year rule on an even more vigorous defense of the interests of capital. In this respect, Abacha played a role similar to that of the early 1990s leaders in Bolivia, Syria, and Venezuela. He cut inflation, built public infrastructure, and increased Nigeria's foreign exchange reserves. He made these moves, of course, to please global capital. At the same time, he undermined any hint of Nigerian democracy or popular rule[217]. He created a massive police state and racked up a terrible human rights record[218].

The military tried again in 1999, holding new elections to return to civilian rule. This time the military found the results more to its liking. It allowed the results to stick, paving the way for the current situation in the country. The People's Democratic Party (PDP) won all elections held from 1999 to 2011, and it governed until 2015. It was the sort of center-right party the military had in mind in 1993. The PDP even governed under a symbolic union of Nigeria's past political forces, running a ticket that combined a former military leader and political prisoner with a former member of the SDP.

However, the PDP lost the 2015 election to the allegedly center-left All Progressives Congress (APC). The APC won re-election in 2019, cementing its status as the ruling party. On the surface, the APC looks similar to Abiola's SDP. It presents a broad ideological coalition, but the coalition notably includes leftist elements. Some of its members are influenced by Nigerian leftists like the social democratic nationalist leader Obafemi Awolowo or the socialist politician Aminu Kano[219]. Indeed, these leaders and their political followers even operate to the left of Abiola and the SDP. As a result, we might have expected military elements to step in, overthrow the APC, and reset Nigerian politics once again. It did not. In fact, the military largely left the APC alone to govern. Why? Are there differences between the SDP and the APC? Why have these differences protected the APC from a coup, especially in light of the fact that the APC contains left-wing elements?

---

[217] See, for example: https://www.refworld.org/docid/3ae6ab4d1c.html; https://1997-2001.state.gov/global/human_rights/1996_hrp_report/nigeria.html. Both last accessed: August 1, 2020.

[218] Interestingly, the U.S. took larger action well after Abacha left office, once he was no longer part of the power structure. See: https://www.justice.gov/opa/pr/us-freezes-more-458-million-stolen-former-nigerian-dictator-largest-kleptocracy-forfeiture. Last accessed: August 1, 2020.

[219] Awolowo was a parliamentarian and government official with politics more nationalist and/or social democratic than socialist. Kano, on the other hand, helped lead socialist and anti-colonialist movements as a young man.

I find two key factors holding the Nigerian military back from a coup. These factors also help explain why the U.S. largely stays out of internal Nigerian affairs. First, as we pointed out above, the APC holds itself together as a *very* broad ideological coalition. It includes the socialist and social democratic elements I mentioned above. But they compose a small part of its base, and they play a role arguably even smaller than their numbers suggest. In addition to these groups, the APC includes a variety of liberal and progressive parties. It also includes moderate and right-wing parties, such as the powerful All Nigeria Peoples Party. Not only does the APC include these parties, but the party's winning presidential candidate himself came from the APC's right-wing elements. And so, far from being a marginal part of the coalition, the APC allows its center-right and right-wing elements great influence. Rather than strong leftist ideology, the APC roots its politics in opposition to the PDP and advocacy for good governance and anti-corruption policies. It's not a group likely to propose a sweeping slate of policies the military opposes. Despite the name 'progressives,' the group appears quite pragmatic and open to governing from any part of the political spectrum.

Second, the APC broke far less from Nigeria's tradition of military rule than one might initially think. Muhammadu Buhari hails from its right-wing elements and holds the presidency, as we noted above. But not only does he find his political origins on the right. In fact, he's deeply entrenched in Nigeria's military structure. Buhari reached the rank of major general by the 1980s, and he overthrew the government in 1983. He maintained alliances with military elements over the years, and he brought those alliances to the APC. This kind of resume enabled him to quickly earn credibility and trust with Nigeria's military. And so, it's highly unlikely the military sees him or his version of the APC as a threat to its status. The APC seems to remain safe from a coup so long as these right-wing elements – or Buhari himself – remain in charge.

The APC, then, operates as a more complex system of alliances than might appear at an initial glance. It has at least some inclination to try to make the world a bit better for Nigerians. But it remains deeply embedded within establishment politics. As a whole, it has no aims to change the underlying economic and political system of Nigeria. While it does have some similarities with the SDP, the military views it as far more 'safe.' It doesn't present even the general, vague threat to the establishment that the SDP posed.

As noted, the APC *does* frame its politics in terms of making the world better for poor and/or marginalized Nigerians. And in office, it *did* advance notable liberal legislation. Buhari launched a National Social Investment Program, for example, in 2016[220]. The APC also made headway on issues of corruption. It tends to focus on corruption cases it can tie directly to the PDP, still the country's main opposition party. This, of course, invites speculation about corruption and electioneering of a different kind. Many of these cases relate to an ongoing campaign against a Boko Haram insurgency, centering on the APC's discovery of evidence of corruption from arms deals the PDC brokered. On the whole, though, the APC has not succeeded in these policies. Social investment did not prevent a rise in unemployment and economic stagnation[221]. This pushed Nigeria to take stronger measures within its limited political boundaries, as we'll see in the following section.

When we review the Nigerian system, we see an overall situation a bit like that of Bolivia and Venezuela in the early 1990s. Bolivia and Venezuela transitioned from less stable, quasi-democratic systems to more democratic ones, as did Nigeria. Nigeria moved from military rule to relatively stable, two-party democracy. Of course, one difference stands out. Unlike in Bolivia and Venezuela, there's no large-scale, leftist electoral movement in Nigeria. Leftists did not organize around Indigenous and post-colonial interests to win power in Nigeria. Nor did Nigeria elect leaders from the anti-colonial resistance movements of the mid-20th century. We find *that* approach in places like Libya or Zimbabwe, examples we could strongly contrast to Nigeria. Rather, Nigeria created a two-party democracy of the sort the U.S. finds appealing. The system responds to some popular interests, but it strictly limits itself to actions

---

[220] See, for example: http://venturesafrica.com/n-power-key-to-delivering-campaign-promise/. Last accessed July 17, 2020.

[221] See Africa Confidential 2016 - https://www.africa-confidential.com/index.aspx?pageid=7&articleid=11829 - for a discussion of some of these economic forces.

that benefit global capital. For the U.S. left, this creates higher barriers to international solidarity. We find a variety of internal leftist groups in places like Bolivia or Venezuela. It's not impossible to find those groups in Nigeria, but it's more difficult. The U.S. left might ask which Nigerian leftist groups could use assistance building power.

Eko Atlantic City and the Clinton Global Initiative

As we discussed above, the U.S. has long been an ally of some kind to Nigeria. It allied itself through the dreaded lens of 'stability' in the region. As we've noted, what the U.S. state and press call 'stability' does not match well with what most people mean by the word. In times of conflict, the U.S. promotes 'stability' by supporting whichever side of the conflict better aligns to U.S. interests. In exchange for friendly policies, the U.S. overlooks most problems and issues with whichever military figure holds power. However, the Nigerian state does not promote only U.S. interests. Rather, it promotes the interests of global capital in general.

When we expand our horizons to include global capital more broadly, we also expand our analytical power. We can look at specific cases of how these interests work together with both mainstream U.S. foreign policy and NGOs and nonprofits. These NGO and nonprofit groups play supporting roles to the Nigerian state *and* to nations with which Nigeria works. Expanding our reach also allows us to draw connections between events in Nigeria and events elsewhere in sub-Saharan Africa. We can thus elaborate on how Nigeria serves as exemplar for the region. It illustrates how the U.S. and global capital apply its policies more broadly. Furthermore, as we'll see, global capital may innovate in Nigeria and export those innovations elsewhere.

We'll look at one such innovation in the case of Eko Atlantic City. Eko Atlantic City is a site where all these interests converge and where global capital develops exportable ideas. It's a project very friendly to global capital, representative of the kind of public-private partnerships that characterize the neoliberal phase of capitalism. It's a kind of public-private partnership that, among other things, uses public resources to create private wealth. The project was founded as a joint effort between the central Nigerian state, the local Lagos government, and a variety of private capital interests. NGOs and nonprofits supported these interests. They stepped in to facilitate in several critical ways, as we'll see below. It serves first and foremost as a good example of primitive accumulation. But it also shows how primitive accumulation in one nation links to ongoing accumulation in other nations. And it shows the central role extractivist policy plays in these systems of accumulation. At this site, the interests of these various groups converge in new and instructive ways.

In a narrow sense, the Eko Atlantic City project centers on reclaiming the sea. By doing this, it adds to Nigeria's land mass around its capital Lagos. But why do Nigeria and global capital want to reclaim the sea? They want to establish a zone of commerce and private capital on the reclaimed land. Furthermore, they have good reasons to think it's profitable to reclaim land at this particular site. The new land sits near a bustling metropolis, for one. But – perhaps more importantly for global capital – the state would exempt the new land from its broad regulatory apparatus. It thus creates a two-tiered system of regulation near Lagos – one set of regulations for current businesses and another set for those nearby. The project also establishes several other forms of commerce. This includes entertainment and gaming sites, hotels, and other tourist attractions. Thus, various forces envision Eko Atlantic City as a site to serve as a haven for capital and tourists. It allows capital broad access to public institutions and the built environment. Capital, of course, needs these things to thrive. But the project doesn't require capital to uphold its end of the social contract. Capital doesn't have to support in turn the institutions that support *it*. Tourists get roughly the same deal. They get all the benefits of a location near a major world city. But they don't face any negative consequences or issues. The capitalist and the tourist, then, scored a major win with Eko Atlantic City.

Katie Jane Fernelius has written and reported extensively on Eko Atlantic City and related Nigerian developments. She based this work in part on her work as a journalist in Lagos during her Fulbright scholarship travel[222]. She discussed this work recently in an article in *Current Affairs*[223]. But for a more extensive discussion, readers should consult her expansive podcast discussion for the BBC World Service[224]. In the podcast, Fernelius and Ishan Thakore – now a television producer – explain the project as one Nigeria built near a commercial area. But Nigeria destroyed a popular beach in the process. It thereby created a physical separation between wealthy tourists and the Nigerian people. Furthermore, the project displaced tens of thousands of Nigerians who lived in the area. It thus destroyed a local community in the service of global capital. Fernelius terms the Eko Atlantic City project a 'private city.' In doing so, she gives it an excellent description. Nigeria built it for the private interests of global capital and its allies. Noteworthy financial and marketing backers of the project include the Clinton Global Initiative[225] and billionaire financiers Gilbert and Ronald Chagoury. These backers – no mere bit players – were essential to the early successes of the project.

The Chagourys bring this project full circle, tying primitive accumulation to ongoing accumulation to extractivism. They built their fortune much earlier in the oil industry. For decades, extractive industries – particularly oil – formed the cornerstone of the Nigerian economy and its plan of development. It also stood out as a major site of power and struggle in the nation. Oil, in particular, stood as the major site of conflict between global capital and the interests of most Nigerians. We might begin with the expectation that an oil baron would become an earlier financier of a project like Eko Atlantic City. It represents what goes on underneath the surface of a utopian, futuristic city project.

---

[222] For Fernelius's bio and brief description of project, see: https://baldwinscholars.duke.edu/content/katie-jane-fernelius. Last accessed June 19, 2020. See even more so: https://katiejanefernelius.com/work. Last accessed June 19, 2020.

[223] https://www.currentaffairs.org/2020/05/a-private-city-the-rise-of-eko-atlantic. Last accessed June 19, 2020.

[224] https://podcasts.apple.com/us/podcast/the-battle-for-the-future-of-lagos/id1437398608?i=1000422756354&mt=2. Last accessed June 19, 2020. As one gathers from listening to the postcast, local attitudes toward Eko Atlantic City were in fact rather mixed.

[225] Due to widespread criticism and other controversies during Hillary Clinton's 2016 presidential campaign, the Clinton Global Initiative began winding down in late 2016 and shut down by early 2017.

But the Clinton Global Initiative played an interesting and subtle role in the Eko Atlantic City project. Indeed, it played a role arguably as important as the one the Chagourys played. It served as the marketing and branding wing of the project. It presented Eko Atlantic City as 'modern' and 'eco-friendly.' Thus, it justified the project mostly in environmental terms, pointing out the fact that the ocean regularly engulfed lands near Lagos. This helped global capital frame the project in terms of the fight against coastal erosion. We might trace the rhetoric of these support operations. The Clinton Global Initiative took a project with major underlying problems and put on it a charitable, friendly public face. In addition to the general environmental concerns with a reclamation project of this size, investigators associated specific problems with Eko Atlantic City. An ocean surge in 2012 caused major damage and killed people near the site[226]. Partners in the project obviously did not want these kinds of stories to dominate the headlines. And so, the Clinton Global Initiative drew attention elsewhere – from the negative impact of finance and global capital to some of its alleged benefits.

The Clinton Global Initiative served as an interesting choice for this work due to its nature as an organization. In some sense, it served as a standard NGO group with the usual charitable and practical purposes. But it linked rather closely to the interests of global capital and the U.S. state. We can read this merely from the projects it involved itself in. But we hardly need to go that far. We can start by pointing out the obvious: a former U.S. President founded it. For that reason alone, it's inevitable people would link it to the interests of capital and the U.S. state. In the U.S. itself, these events turned into a minor scandal but a largely forgotten one. They presented minor problems for Hillary Clinton during her time as Secretary of State and as a candidate for the presidency. The work had a greater impact on Nigeria. For the U.S. left, the case serves as a clear example of where the interests of global capital, NGOs, nonprofits, and the state meld. At specific sites, these interests merge, overlap, and move forward together. And so, we must keep watch over seemingly charitable

---

[226] https://allafrica.com/stories/201208190103.html. Last accessed June 19, 2020.

or nonprofit groups. Placed in a context of global capital and developing states, they may serve interests less wholesome than previously thought.

This also serves as another area where the U.S. left should take a different approach from the one Michael Walzer advocates. We saw in previous chapters areas where Walzer took too friendly an attitude toward U.S. policy in Israel and in other sites of conflict. Here I think Walzer advocates for a policy too friendly to NGOs. In his discussion of Syria, Walzer argues the left should show solidarity with Syrian dissident and leftist groups[227]. But when explaining what left internationalism looks like in practice, Walzer fails to go beyond NGOs based in liberal values. He particularly advocates for established groups like Human Rights Watch and Amnesty International. Some of these groups do fine work, but they do not build the kind of working-class solidarity that create and sustain leftist movements. Indeed, Walzer disavows class politics, explicitly including upper middle-income professionals as important parts of these 'solidarity' campaigns[228]. While these kinds of NGOs are fine, they cannot form the core of a left international solidarity movement. We see in the case of Eko Atlantic City the limits of NGO work divorced from class analysis, class politics, and popular agency. The U.S. left must build its own organizations based on its own democratic and participatory values. It must build direct links with working-class people around the globe.

Nigeria, The U.S., and Fighting Global Capital

U.S. policy in Nigeria closely tracks U.S. policy in the broader sub-Saharan Arica region. The U.S. is more likely to fight outright wars in the Middle East, even when it pursues extractivist policies in both regions. It sees in the Middle East more peer nations and rivals than it does in sub-Saharan Africa. And the U.S. is more likely to fight over electoral coalitions in Latin American nations like Bolivia and Venezuela than it is in sub-Saharan Africa. While we might appeal to many possible causes, the proximity of Latin America stands out. We don't have anything in Africa comparable to the Monroe Doctrine. And so, at a broad level the

---

[227] Walzer 2018, pp. 5-7.
[228] Ibid., p. 49.

U.S. fights wars in the Middle East and meddles in Latin American elections. It tends to focus its policy in a different way in Nigeria and the rest of sub-Saharan Africa.

The U.S. treats Nigeria as a nation at the early stages of capitalist development. Accordingly, it focuses its policy around primitive accumulation. And it promotes these forces through alliances between the U.S. and Nigerian state, global capital, and NGO and nonprofit groups. The alliance aims at the extraction of resources, the promotion of finance capital, and the public and private infrastructure capital needs to do these things. As a starting point, the U.S. left must analyze and promote knowledge of these alliances and what they're doing. It can use this knowledge to build better international solidarity campaigns. These campaigns must work outside of the influence of global capital and its affiliate groups and allies.

We live in a world of uneven development and stages. The U.S. and Nigeria did not develop capitalist systems at the same time or always in the same way. And so, they relate to one another on a different footing. Primitive accumulation in Nigeria relates to accumulation by other and ongoing means in the U.S. and Europe. These latter forms of accumulation – as Harvey lays them out, as we saw earlier – focus on privatizing state and/or public assets. All these forces stretch beyond any single nation, political party, or elected government. They marshal the resources of many supporting groups. And the familiar bipartisan foreign policy consensus in the U.S. serves their aims. But we find a difference between all this and oil wars in the Middle East or coups in Latin America. Much of what the U.S. does in Nigeria doesn't look obviously problematic or scary on the surface. Sometimes it even looks like real developmental or humanitarian aid. The slick marketing presentations of the NGOs convince many people – even some leftists. NGOs soften the rough edges of foreign policy in the mind of the public. They even appeal to progressive values. And they do so in ways analogous to how the Democratic Party does so in domestic U.S. politics.

This situation leaves the U.S. left with many challenges and lessons. We must build a foreign policy operation to address them. We must create groups democratic and robust enough to effectively counter global capital.

Ideally, groups will work closely and directly with ordinary Nigerians. And to do so, they may have to work around NGOs and nonprofits. This presents many challenges. For our primary lesson as leftists, we need to connect the situation on the ground to the fight against global capital. Global capital built a complex project in Nigeria, one that puts together many allies and affiliate organizations. The fight against the project includes fighting on multiple fronts. By learning about these fronts, we can better direct our efforts to build popular coalitions against global capital.

Let's compare the situation in Nigeria to the one in China. U.S. companies incorporate China into their global supply chains. They often hide these links. But with analytical and solidarity work, we can uncover the links. And then we can build the right alliances and groups to fight global capital. In Nigeria, global capital even more thoroughly hides the links. It doesn't simply link together different parts of a global supply chain, but rather, it builds ties with separate proxy groups. It creates alliances with groups that have no apparent or obvious economic role in the region. And it uses Nigeria as a site of early accumulation and theft rather than as a link in a developed production system. Global capital builds wealth in Nigeria in many ways, and it does so via the production of goods and services in only some cases. Often it goes to Nigeria merely to conduct financial business. These links between finance and global capital are even more difficult to unearth and fight than the ones involved in global supply chains. To do so requires the U.S. left to even more thoroughly build awareness and alliances.

Conclusion

Much of the U.S. political left had a political awakening in 2019 and 2020. Between the Bernie Sanders presidential campaign and the racial justice demonstrations and protests, the left raised consciousness and interest surged. Our greatest challenge is to expand and channel this interest into useful strategies and projects. And the way to accomplish these things is to *organize*. While the new ideas and energy are encouraging, many new leftists – especially young leftists – don't know where to begin. New leftists – including many readers of this book – are worried about the future, but they don't yet know how to change it. They want to get started, but they don't know where to turn. Collectively, we know we want to build a movement and win.

I hope readers take from this book some of the ideas and tools they need to move from where they are to where they want to be. In particular, readers should now be able to see the role foreign policy plays in this, especially the importance of international solidarity. In the process of adding foreign policy to our domestic policy consensus, we gain new sources for action and growth. We develop new ways to connect with people around the globe. And these connections make even our domestic politics more effective and sustainable. We can take from international solidarity movements some of the lessons we need to organize better movements in the U.S. And then we can put these things together to work for a more pluralistic world and winnable fights against global capital – hand-in-hand with leftists from many nations.

We'll finish our discussion by focusing on two topics. First, we'll look at a couple of the more difficult cases in U.S. foreign policy: U.S. wars in Afghanistan in 2000s and Serbia in the late 1990s. We'll use these cases to sharpen the skills learned earlier in the book, and these cases will provide readers with a helpful guide to evaluating future cases. By sharpening our analytical tools on these more difficult cases, we can apply the lessons to new and ongoing foreign policy issues. Second, we'll discuss some very concrete steps new and young leftists can take to build better movements. I'll lay out several steps readers can begin implementing right away. By implementing these steps, readers can learn how to better organize. And the best way to learn is through doing.

Afghanistan, Serbia, and War

It's easy to condemn the U.S. for what it did in the war in Iraq. It's also quite pertinent. U.S. leftists universally oppose the war. But many progressives and liberals *also* oppose the war – even a few conservatives do, too. Yes, some of the same liberals voted for it in 2003, but even in those days the war garnered significant liberal opposition and more than a few liberal votes against it. For these reasons, we can't organize a leftist foreign policy around cases like the war in Iraq. Iraq stands out as such an outrageous example of U.S. imperialism that even many non-leftists see the problem. To carve out a specifically leftist foreign policy space – to see what the left adds to foreign policy discussion – we must look beyond these cases toward more difficult ones.

That's why we focused in Chapters 4-7 on nations where the U.S. imposes empire and hegemony in more subtle ways. We discussed seemingly humanitarian interventions, political interference, and other actions not usually involving troop deployment. And for these same reasons, I'd like to add to the conclusion a discussion of two cases that *do* involve troop deployment: U.S. wars in Afghanistan and the former Yugoslavia. There were seemingly noble reasons for the U.S. to invade these places – Afghanistan in the early 2000s and the former Yugoslavia in the late 1990s. While Iraq struck leftists as a transparent war for oil, some thought the U.S. had plausible justice and humanitarian grounds for entering these other nations. The cases of Afghanistan and the former Yugoslavia will sharpen our analytical tools, provide additional support for our principle of anti-interventionism, and allow us to proactively address new cases.

The Afghani government likely harbored the people who planned and supported the 9/11 terrorist attacks on New York and Washington. Furthermore, the Afghani government had a long history of religious extremism and religion-inspired oppression of its population, particularly Afghani women. In the former Yugoslavia, the Serbian state sent its military to fight a separatist movement in Kosovo. President Slobodan Milošević was also linked by the U.S. to earlier human rights violations in Bosnia, though the International Court of Justice cleared him of this latter charge after his death. The U.S. thus justified the NATO-led invasion of Kosovo and the Serbian state in humanitarian terms. Some prominent leftists, including Michael Walzer, thought this was all enough to justify the U.S. invasions. They saw problems they believed the U.S. – even in its present form – could address productively. They were wrong about this.

We can use our four basic principles to evaluate these thornier cases. As a starting point, our principles give us good reasons for skepticism toward the U.S. invasions. First, any U.S. invasion involves the use of U.S. power, and a successful invasion increases that power. And so, we should begin by setting a high bar for when we approve of U.S. invasions. We should weigh each case very carefully, because even when an invasion 'succeeds' it often has greater negative impact than positive impact. Rather than beginning from a place of neutrality, we should begin by putting the onus on defenders of invasions. Defenders of invasion should be able to show clearly how the likely benefits of U.S. action weigh heavier than the regrettable increase in U.S. power that results.

Second, the U.S. press significantly distorted the facts in both Afghanistan and Kosovo. In Afghanistan, the press played down the role of international institutions and international options for settling the conflict. The press dismissed out of hand the possibility of using the international justice system to apprehend and try the planners of 9/11 as criminals rather than as military targets[229]. They also quickly dismissed negotiations between President George W. Bush and Afghani leader

---

[229] Michael Walzer, whose work we discussed extensively in Chapter 2, also dismisses this possibility. But see Vine 2020, p. 269 and p. 307, for a review of evidence showing that treating terrorists as criminals is more effective than treating them as military targets.

Mullah Mohammed Omar. This provided political cover for Bush when he quickly wrote off those negotiations as a failure. Perhaps in better circumstances the negotiations could have succeeded. Furthermore, even if the U.S. chose to take military action – an option it never demonstrated as necessary – it could have undertaken a smaller-scale raid or operation. The press never seriously discussed this possibility. In Kosovo, the U.S. press uncritically accepted the U.S. version of events. It accepted all the charges against Milošević, even the ones later overturned by the ICJ. It also repeatedly accepted Bill Clinton and Tony Blair's reversal of the timeline, failing to note that Milošević ramped up his human rights violations *after* the threat of invasion rather than *before*. Thus, many of the human rights violations later used as a justification for the war were a *result* of the war rather than a *reason* for it[230]. And so, it's quite likely U.S./NATO action increased the danger of the situation, at least in the short-term.

Third, there's a deep history of failed foreign invasion in both nations, but particularly Afghanistan. The Soviet Union invaded Afghanistan in the late 1970s and 1980s, largely failing to achieve its objectives and causing thousands of deaths. Prior NATO-led intervention in Yugoslavia in the early 1990s – as it was breaking apart into multiple nations – was also notably less than a stunning success, both in terms of results and in terms of the accuracy of information coming from the region. These failures were not a major part of the conversation in mainstream U.S. politics at the time. It's almost as though lack of success in the past is no stumbling block in the U.S. toward advocacy for largely similar proposals in the future. This provides us with educational opportunities as leftists.

In both cases, the U.S. left must weigh various benefits and harms. We must compare the likely harm done by the invasion with the potential for the invasion to do good. But that's not exactly a neutral comparison. We must begin by reminding ourselves what U.S. invasions are like and how the U.S. actually forms its foreign policy goals, not the goals we *want* it to have. U.S. invasions are often unsuccessful and often involve killing tens of thousands of people, sometimes millions, e.g., Vietnam. Furthermore,

---

[230] See, for example, https://chomsky.info/200005__/. Last accessed: October 28, 2020.

the U.S. is an imperial and hegemonic power concerned primarily with promoting its own interests, with humanitarian goals always secondary to that primary goal. Thus, there's strong potential in any given case for the U.S. to fail or to leave the world worse off than it found it.

In light of all this background, there's little justification for the invasion of Afghanistan. While my own politics weren't terribly developed at the time, I don't think anyone was wrong to join the Bloomington Peace Camp against the war in Afghanistan in 2001-2002. Whether their methods were the right ones – or whether they supported the anti-war movement for the right reasons – the actual results were spot-on. Furthermore, I think we can draw the same conclusion in the Serbia case. There were significant problems with the U.S. operation, both in terms of its methods and (lack of) potential to do good. The end results in Serbia were perhaps better than Afghanistan, but the U.S. left had significant reason to oppose both operations. The history of U.S. foreign policy we've reviewed in this book presents us with many reasons for skepticism about these operations as well as many reasons to remain unsurprised at the largely negative results. Many Americans – even foreign policy experts – profess surprise at the bad results. But on a careful examination, they should have expected those results.

One might ask, of course: is there *ever* a justified war for the U.S., or for any imperial and/or hegemonic power? Should the U.S. left embrace outright pacifism? We briefly considered these questions in Chapter 2, and – as I said in that discussion – I don't think we need a completely worked-out theory of just wars. But, for now, I'm not arguing for pacifism, even in the case of an imperial or hegemonic power. I suspect there are some cases of advisable U.S. wars, but they're few and far between. We might consider something like a global fascist threat, such as Nazi Germany. If there were such a threat in the future, then I think we could make a good case for a U.S. invasion of the global fascist power. It would be a useful exercise for readers to take up some of these questions in more depth in their own thoughts and in their own leftist organizations and discussion groups.

One thing to note here, of course, is that these are all thorny cases of war. But, as we've emphasized throughout this book, major foreign policy issues stretch well beyond war. Most everyday foreign policy issues are about things like international trade, arms sales, diplomatic efforts, foreign aid, and others. I'm discussing, of course, cases like the ones we examined in Chapters 4-7. But we can use these principles and these discussions to help evaluate those other cases, too. Who's really being served by *that* trade deal or arms sale? Why is the U.S. sending aid to *that* country? How central are professed humanitarian interests to the real reasons? These are the kinds of questions leftists should ask themselves and one another when deciding whether specific foreign policy moves are good ones we should support.

What's a Leftist to Do?

What can new and young leftists do *now*, at the earliest stages of political organizing? Many leftists were energized by the Bernie Sanders campaign – 2016, 2020, or both – but don't necessarily have a next step in mind. Many leftists were energized by the Black Lives Matter movement, by the pressing need for racial justice, good health care, a satisfying job that pays a living wage, and other things. And still other leftists were energized by the things they see the U.S. doing overseas, by the ways the U.S. supports coups and invades other nations. What steps can they take? Our basic principles and the discussion of cases in Part II provide us with a roadmap of how to get involved through organizing.

In my view, the first and most important step is to join an organization working along explicitly socialist lines. And in the U.S., the obvious best candidate right now is the Democratic Socialists of America. It's not that it's the only group. It isn't. It's not even that it's the best group, ideologically. For a long time, in fact, the DSA stood out as one of the less ideologically solid organizations on the U.S. left. It has a long history of doing things like endorsing John Kerry for President or failing to challenge the political status quo through on the ground activism or strategic campaign building. But the DSA has strong advantages over other organizations that make it the best choice. For one, it has far more members than any other socialist group in the U.S. in decades. If readers want to find like-minded people to help build a leftist future, the DSA is the best place to find those people. Second, the DSA has significant resources to help connect people and get them started. Building connections with fellow leftists is the most important step organizers need to take, and the DSA stands alone as the best place in the U.S. to build those connections. From there, leftists can join or start all sorts of organizing campaigns. The Iowa City Tenants Union – a group I discussed earlier – was itself founded by the Iowa City local chapter of the DSA. A group like the DSA provides the most potential social connections and widest range of ways to get involved.

A second step leftists can take – this one specifically on foreign policy – is to start a foreign policy book group and/or discussion group. While this may seem too 'academic' to some – and possibly too 'detached' to many – there are many ways to start an effective discussion group that's neither of those things. Readers shouldn't sweat too much over *which* book to read. You can read an introductory book like this one, or you can read books tackling in more depth the history of imperialism and colonialism. Or you can read in-depth discussion of particular conflicts and wars. These questions are entirely up to the participants, and there are no hard and fast rules on how to do it best.

More important than the book you read is how you run the group. As we've seen in earlier chapters, the discussion leader doesn't have to be an expert on the topic or even especially well-read on it. They need to be good at getting people together and promoting discussion. At the same time, discussion leaders shouldn't make it all *too* open-ended. They shouldn't just assign readings and expect everyone to be able to come to the discussion with questions without some guidance and prompting. In this situation, many won't do the reading, and even the ones who do the reading won't have much to say about it. For a good book group, the discussion leader assigns a manageable reading load and starts the group members with some questions to consider as they read. And then ask them to come to the meeting with a question or two in mind. Some will rephrase the questions they're given at the outset, but they'll have better framing and perspective on it. And still others will come up with their own questions, but they'll have better guidance along the way.

Third, and perhaps most important, leftists should directly connect as much as possible with leftists in other countries[231]. This especially goes for countries that have experimented in the last couple of decades with leftist governance. We discussed several examples in earlier chapters, notably Venezuela and Bolivia. This is a good 'advanced' assignment for people who have already joined DSA, started discussion groups and other groups, and who have built up some background knowledge on U.S. foreign policy. But it's also a step people can take at earlier stages. Readers can find leftists who currently live in Bolivia, Venezuela, or the Middle East. They can find leftists from these places who immigrated to the U.S. They can connect through social media or school, or they can connect through a DSA meeting or DSA caucus. There are lots of ways to connect, and readers – especially young readers – probably know about more options and possibilities than I do! I've mentioned some of these organizations in the relevant chapters of Part II, but this list is by its nature incomplete. Readers would be well advised to find ways to connect these organizations and their social connections to workplace organizing or a DSA reading group or political education group.

Finally, readers – and new and young leftists of all kinds – should treat people with respect. Lots of people are interested in leftist ideas and leftist groups. Organizations like the DSA have new and curious people showing up to meetings all the time. These first impressions and contacts are particularly important. Many interested people have specific issues they're *very* worried about or specific approaches, but they don't necessarily have a deep leftist background. They'll make mistakes. They don't know many of the seemingly 101-level stuff even lots of readers of this book will already know. That's all okay. Leftists need to build a movement, not a small club. It's not about being ideologically perfect or flawless. It's not about never making mistakes. We need people to join and learn, and getting people to join and learn involves supporting our comrades as they learn and grow.

---

[231] See Nagajara 2020 for a few good examples of organizations building these kinds of connections. He points, for example, to the Grassroots Global Justice Alliance, which is a coalition of organizations working specifically on working-class connections between the U.S. and South America.

I often think back to that conversation I had with an Iowa caucus-goer in February 2020. She's exactly the kind of person we need to join the DSA and work toward a bigger leftist movement. She's the kind of person we need to knock on doors, meet new people, develop ideas, fight landlords and bosses, and build more power together with fellow working-class people. Leftists can learn how to have discussions like this. And while doing so they can distinguish between leftist and liberal ideas while also treating people with respect and dignity. Many people like her wander into a meeting of groups like the DSA. They're curious, and they want to make a difference. Maybe they join the meeting on a whim, having heard little about the organization other than that it's a group of people working on something better. Maybe they were involved in local advocacy or advocacy for a policy like Medicare for All. And maybe they even have some guarded skepticism or reservations about the group, especially if they're familiar with some of the acrimonious discussion over the Elizabeth Warren campaign or over some of the internal harassment problems within certain DSA chapters. Regardless of where individuals begin, leftists need a way to engage in first discussions, first steps along the road toward becoming part of a broader movement.

I hope this book helps readers take these steps themselves and guide others through these steps.

Postscript

This book grew from my leftist activist work. We talk about current events in my DSA chapter meetings. Inevitably, at least one person mentions a foreign policy issue – almost always an issue of war and peace. Ears perk up. People are interested. But they don't really know how to get started or how to take action. I hope they now have enough material to get started.

I completed the writing over the course of 2020, starting a bit before the pandemic and continuing until the final days of the Trump Administration. This made for challenging work – not just due to the stress of living through a pandemic, but also because organizing changed. In the DSA, we had to shift all our meetings to online-only. And in the Iowa City Tenants Union, we had to organize tenants and pressure landlords without the kinds of close, in-person conversations that form the core of good organizing work. So far, I've been able to apply organizing lessons and principles to online organizing. But we had to adapt our work and find new ways to make it accessible to a wide range of people.

Finally, for me, writing is about a sense of place. I do most of my work in coffee shops, including both my Ph.D dissertation and first book. That plan obviously didn't work for *this* book. I integrated home and place in much different – and much more literal – ways. I wrote most of this book at my desk in my home in Iowa City – alone, due to a family medical issue – surrounded by books and houseplants. But I found other ways to integrate home and place. For example, this book is written in a font called Iowan Old Style – invented right here in Iowa City. The pandemic forced us to adapt in our own ways.

Acknowledgements

Each book involves a wide range of people. This one comes from hundreds of conversations, meetings, happy hours, and readings.

Thanks first and foremost to all the people in the Iowa City Democratic Socialists of America and Iowa City Tenants Union who took part in those discussions. I can't list everyone, but here are many of the people who stand out: Alison Clark, Derick Delloro, Alex Loehrer, Michael Rack, Rob Shaw, and Laura Widman.

Finally, a special thanks to Andrea Truitt for being a wonderful partner, reader of this book, and life companion.

References

Abbott, Jared and Dustin Guastella. 2019. "A Socialist Party in Our Time?" in Catalyst, Vol. 3, No. 2, pp. 7-63.

Ally, Shireen and Arianna Lissoni. 2017. New Histories of South Africa's Apartheid-Era Bantustans. Routledge: New York.

Appy, Christian G. 2019. "Empire Lite," in Catalyst, Vol. 3, No. 3, pp. 133-153.

Awad, Sumaya and brian bean, eds. 2020. Palestine: A Socialist Introduction. Haymarket Books: Chicago.

Bacevich, Andrew. 2004. American Empire: The Realities and Consequences of US Diplomacy. Harvard University Press: Cambridge. 2013. Breach of Trust: How Americans Failed Their Solders and Their Country. Metropolitan Books: New York.

Bloodworth, James 2018. Hired: Six Months Undercover in Low-Wage Britain. Atlantic Books: London.

Bradbury, Alexandra, Mark Brenner, and Jane Slaughter. 2016. Secrets of a Successful Organizer. A Labor Notes Book: Detroit, MI.

Brownlee, Jason. 2021. "Shadow Wars and Corporate Welfare," in Catalyst, Vol. 4, No. 4, pp. 95-121.

Carter, Jimmy. 2006. Palestine: Peace Not Apartheid. Simon & Schuster: New York.

Chen, Michelle. 2020. "On Immigration: A Socialist Case for Open Borders," in Kate Aronoff, Peter Dreier, and Michael Kazin (eds.), We Own the Future: Democratic Socialism—American Style. The New Press, New York: 2020, pp. 177-189.

Chomsky, Noam. 2014 [1983]. Fateful Triangle: The United States, Israel, and the Palestinians. Haymarket Books: Chicago.

Ciccariello-Maher, George. 2013. We Created Chávez: A People's History of the Venezuelan Revolution. Duke University Press.

Coates, Ta-Nehisi. 2017. We Were Eight Years in Power: An American Tragedy. One World: New York.

Cowie, Jefferson 2001. Capital Moves: RCA's Seventy-Year Quest for Cheap Labor. The New Press: New York.

Darden, Jessica Trisko. 2020. Aiding and Abetting: U.S. Foreign Assistance and State Violence. Stanford University Press: Stanford.

Davis, Angela Y. 2016. Freedom is a Constant Struggle: Ferguson, Palestine, and the Foundations of a Movement. Edited by Frank Barat. Haymarket Books: Chicago.

Day, Meagan and Micah Uetricht. 2020. Bigger Than Bernie: How We Go From the Sanders Campaign to Democratic Socialism. Verso: New York.

deBoer, Fredrik. 2020. The Cult of Smart: How Our Broken Education System Perpetuates Social Injustice. All Points Books: New York.

Drabek, Matt L. 2014. Classify and Label: The Unintentional Marginalization of Social Groups. Lexington Books: Lanham, MD.
2020. A Primer on Trumpism: Understanding and Fighting the U.S. Far-Right. Kindle Edition. https://www.amazon.com/dp/B08HSM6HRR.
2021. Capitalism's Heart Surgeon: Elizabeth Warren and the Progressive Movement. Kindle Edition. https://www.amazon.com/dp/B08W44XRM5.

Feldman, David B. 2020. "The Question of Borders," in Catalyst: Volume 4, No. 1., pp. 147-181.

Fischbach, Michael R. 2018. Black Power and Palestine: Transnational Countries of Color. Stanford University Press.

Golinger, Eva. 2005. The Chavez Code: Cracking U.S. Intervention in Venezuela. Olive Branch Press: Northampton, MA.

Gomez-Barris, Macarena. 2018. Beyond the Pink Tide: Art and Political Undercurrents in the Americas. University of California Press.

Gonzalez, Mike. 2018. The Ebb of the Pink Tide: The Decline of the Left in Latin America. Pluto Press: London.

Gopal, Anand. 2020. "The Arab Thermidor," in Catalyst: Volume 4, No. 2, pp. 85-137.

Gopalan, Arparna. 2020. "Taking Class War Global," in Current Affairs: Volume 5, No. 5, pp. 21-26.

Harvey, David. 2010. A Companion to Marx's Capital. Verso: London.
2013. A Companion to Marx's Capital, Volume 2. Verso: London.
2018 [1982]. The Limits to Capital. Verso: London.

Immerwahr, Daniel. 2019. How to Hide an Empire: A History of the Greater United States. Farrar, Straus and Giroux: New York.

Joplin, Ty. 2020. "Scandinavian Solidarity," in Current Affairs: Volume 5, Issue, 2, pp. 12-17.

Kendi, Ibram X. 2017. Stamped from the Beginning: The Definitive History of Racist Ideas in America. Bold Type Books: New York.

Lee, Barbara. 2008. Renegade for Peace & Justice: Congresswoman Barbara Lee Speaks for Me. Rowman & Littlefield: Lanham, MD.

Lee, Suzy. 2019. "The Case for Open Borders," in Catalyst: Volume 2. No. 4, pp. 7-38.
    2020. "Socialists and Immigration," in Catalyst: Volume 4, No. 1, pp. 185-207.
    2021. "Immigration Strategy in the Biden Era," in Catalyst: Vol. 4, No. 4, pp. 73-91.

Maravankin, Stephanie. 2017. "Arab Feminism in the Arab Spring: Discourses on Solidarity, the Socio-Cultural Revolution, and the Political Revolutions in Egypt, Tunisia, and Yemen," in Clocks and Clouds: Vol. 7, No. 2.

Marx, Karl. 1990 [1867]. Capital: Volume I. Trans. Ben Fowkes. Penguin Classics: London.
    1992 [1885]. Capital: Volume II. Trans. David Fernbach. Penguin Classics: London.

McAlevey, Jane. 2018. No Shortcuts: Organizing for Power in the New Guilded Age. Oxford University Press: New York.

Mearsheimer, John J. and Stephen M. Walt. 2008. The Israel Lobby and U.S. Foreign Policy. Farrar, Straus and Giroux: New York.

Moody, Kim. 2017. On New Terrain: How Capital is Reshaping the Battleground of Class War. Haymarket Books: Chicago.

Nagaraja, Tejasvi. 2020. "On Foreign Policy: War from Above, Solidarity from Below," in Kate Aronoff, Peter Dreier, and Michael Kazin (eds.), We Own the Future: Democratic Socialism—American Style. The New Press, New York: 2020, pp. 190-203.

Olin Wright, Erik. 2010. Envisioning Real Utopias. Verso: London. 2019. How to Be an Anticapitalist in the 21st Century. Verso: London.

Pearlman, Wendy. 2017. We Crossed a Bridge and It Trembled: Voices From Syria. HarperCollins: New York.

Piven, Frances Fox and Richard A. Cloward. 1979 [1977]. Poor People's Movements: Why They Succeed, How They Fail. Vintage Books: New York.

Power-Greene, Ousmane. 2014. Against Wind and Tide: The African American Struggle Against the Colonization Movement. NYU Press: New York.

Riofrancos, Thea 2020. Resource Radicals: From Petro-Nationalism to Post-Extractivism in Ecuador. Duke University Press.

Robinson, Nathan J. 2019. Why You Should Be a Socialist. All Points Books: New York.

Rojas, René. 2018. "The Latin American Left's Shifting Tides," in Catalyst, Vol. 2, No. 2, pp. 7-71.

Said, Edward. 1996. Peace and Its Discontents: Essays on Palestine in the Middle East Peace Process. Vintage Books: New York.

Smucker, Jonathan Matthew. 2017. Hegemony How-To: A Roadmap for Radicals. AK Press: Chico, CA.

Striffler, Steve. 2019. Solidarity: Latin America and the US Left in the Era of Human Rights. Pluto Press: London.

Sunkara, Bhaskar, ed. 2016. The ABCs of Socialism. Verso: London.
2019. The Socialist Manifesto: The Case for Radical Politics in an Era of Extreme Inequality. Basic Books: New York.

Veltmeyer, Henry and James Petras. 2014. The New Extractivism: A Post-Neoliberal Development Model or Imperialism of the Twenty-First Century? Zed Books: New York.

Vine, David. 2020. The United States of War: A Global History of America's Endless Conflicts, From Columbus to the Islamic State. University of California Press: Oakland, CA.

Walzer, Michael. 2015 [1977]. Just and Unjust Wars: A Moral Argument with Historical Illustrations. 5th edition. Basic Books: New York.
2018. A Foreign Policy for the Left. Yale University Press: New Haven.

Wilpert, Gregory. 2007. Changing Venezuela By Taking Power: The History and Politics of the Chávez Government. Verso: London.

About the Author

Matt Drabek is a blogger and the Secretary-Treasurer of the Iowa City chapter of Democratic Socialists of America. He also works as a non-profit education professional. He is the author of *Classify and Label: The Unintended Marginalization of Social Groups*.

He has spent the last two decades organizing people to build a better world and analyzing social problems and solutions. His organizing experience stretches from the fair trade and anti-war movements of the early 2000s to more recent work with the Iowa City Tenants Union and the DSA. He was trained as an analytic philosopher, and he uses that training in all aspects of his work. You can find out more about him and his work at the *Base and Superstructure* blog at https://baseandsuperstructure.com.